Michael Corry, PhD
Chih-Hsiung Tu, PhD
Editor

What Works Well

Distance Education: What Works Well has been co-published simultaneously as *Computers in the Schools*, Volume 20, Number 3 2003.

Pre-publication
REVIEWS,
COMMENTARIES,
EVALUATIONS . . .

"A MUST READ. . . . Provides a highly readable, practical, yet critical perspective into the design, delivery, and implementation of distance learning. . . . Examines issues faced by distance educators, offers valuable tactics culled from experience, and outlines strategies that have been key success factors for a wide variety of distance learning initiatives."

Veena Mahesh, PhD
Distance and Blended Learning
Program Manager
Technology Manufacturing
Group Training, Intel Corporation

More pre-publication
REVIEWS, COMMENTARIES, EVALUATIONS . . .

"**O**FFERS COMPREHENSIVE RESOURCES FOR ONLINE K-12 EDUCATORS who wish to deliver quality e-learning instruction. The authors address the design, development, and implementation of student learning experiences, online technologies, and effective teaching strategies. . . . In addition, they include many 'real-life' examples and best practices from different distance education settings with useful 'how-to' guides for online course developers. OF INTEREST TO ADMINISTRATORS, INSTRUCTORS, TECHNOLOGY COORDINATORS, AND EDUCATIONAL RESEARCHERS."

Mei-Yau Shih, PhD
Coordinator of Teaching Technologies
Center for Teaching
University of Massachusetts, Amherst

"**I**NFORMATIVE, THOUGHT PROVOKING, and generally optimistic. . . . Educators and trainers are beset with an avalanche of innovations sweeping over them.

Without a rational analysis as to their efficacy, many will drown. Corry and Tu have thrown you your personal life preserver by assembling AN ALL-STAR CAST OF PROFESSIONALS, both thinkers and doers, to tempt you to move from one work to that which follows. Atsusi Hirumi's diagrams, figures, and appendices alone, are worth the price of this book, as are David Winograd's extensive suggestions related to online conferencing."

Richard A. Cornell, EdD
Professor Emeritus, Instructional Systems, University of Central Florida

"**B**OTH TEACHERS AND STUDENTS WILL BENEFIT. . . . An overview of the various aspects of Internet mediated distance education. Of particular interest, the text discusses the implementation of strategies as well as successes and challenges of distance education in the K–12 environment–a quickly growing methodology in public education."

J. Michael Blocher, PhD
Assistant Professor of Educational Technology, Northern Arizona University

The Haworth Press, Inc.

Distance Education: What Works Well

Distance Education: What Works Well has been co-published simultaneously as *Computers in the Schools*, Volume 20, Number 3 2003.

The *Computers in the Schools* Monographic "Separates"

Below is a list of "separates," which in serials librarianship means a special issue simultaneously published as a special journal issue or double-issue *and* as a "separate" hardbound monograph. (This is a format which we also call a "DocuSerial.")

"Separates" are published because specialized libraries or professionals may wish to purchase a specific thematic issue by itself in a format which can be separately cataloged and shelved, as opposed to purchasing the journal on an on-going basis. Faculty members may also more easily consider a "separate" for classroom adoption.

"Separates" are carefully classified separately with the major book jobbers so that the journal tie-in can be noted on new book order slips to avoid duplicate purchasing.

You may wish to visit Haworth's website at . . .

http://www.HaworthPress.com

. . . to search our online catalog for complete tables of contents of these separates and related publications.

You may also call 1-800-HAWORTH (outside US/Canada: 607-722-5857), or Fax 1-800-895-0582 (outside US/Canada: 607-771-0012), or e-mail at:

docdelivery@haworthpress.com

Distance Education: What Works Well, edited by Michael Corry, PhD, and Chih-Hsiung Tu, PhD (Vol. 20, No. 3, 2003). *"A must read. . . . Provides a highly readable, practical, yet critical perspective into the design, delivery, and implementation of distance learning. . . . Examines issues faced by distance educators, offers valuable tactics culled from experience, and outlines strategies that have been key success factors for a wide variety of distance learning initiatives." (Veena Mahesh, PhD, Distance and Blended Learning Program Manager, Technology Manufacturing Group Training, Intel Corporation)*

Technology in Education: A Twenty-Year Retrospective, edited by D. LaMont Johnson, PhD, and Cleborne D. Maddux, PhD (Vol. 20, No. 1/2, 2003). *"Interesting, informative, relevant. . . . Having so many experts between the covers of one book was a treat. . . . I enjoyed reading this book!" (Susan W. Brown, PhD, Science/Math Methods Professor and Professional Curriculum Coordinator, New Mexico State University)*

Distance Education: Issues and Concerns, edited by Cleborne D. Maddux, PhD, Jacque Ewing-Taylor, MS, and D. LaMont Johnson, PhD (Vol. 19, No. 3/4, 2002). *Provides practical, research-based advice on distance education course design.*

Evaluation and Assessment in Educational Information Technology, edited by Leping Liu, PhD, D. LaMont Johnson, PhD, Cleborne D. Maddux, PhD, and Norma J. Henderson, MS (Vol. 18, No. 2/3 and 4, 2001). *Explores current trends, issues, strategies, and methods of evaluation and assessment in educational information technology.*

The Web in Higher Education: Assessing the Impact and Fulfilling the Potential, edited by Cleborne D. Maddux, PhD, and D. LaMont Johnson, PhD (Vol. 17, No. 3/4 and Vol. 18, No. 1, 2001). *"I enthusiastically recommend this book to anyone new to Web-based program development. I am certain that my project has moved along more rapidly because of what I learned from this text. The chapter on designing online education courses helped to organize my programmatic thinking. Another chapter did an outstanding job of debunking the myths regarding Web learning." (Carol Swift, PhD, Associate Professor and Chair of the Department of Human Development and Child Studies, Oakland University, Rochester, Michigan)*

Using Information Technology in Mathematics Education, edited by D. James Tooke, PhD, and Norma Henderson, MS (Vol. 17, No. 1/2, 2001). *"Provides thought-provoking material on several aspects and levels of mathematics education. The ideas presented will provide food for thought for the reader, suggest new methods for the classroom, and give new ideas for further research." (Charles E. Lamb, EdD, Professor, Mathematics Education, Department of Teaching, Learning, and Culture, College of Education, Texas A&M University, College Station)*

Integration of Technology into the Classroom: Case Studies, edited by D. LaMont Johnson, PhD, Cleborne D. Maddux, PhD, and Leping Liu, PhD (Vol. 16, No. 2/3/4, 2000). *Use these fascinating case studies to understand why bringing information technology into your classroom can make you a more effective teacher, and how to go about it!*

Information Technology in Educational Research and Statistics, edited by Leping Liu, PhD, D. LaMont Johnson, PhD, and Cleborne D. Maddux, PhD (Vol. 15, No. 3/4, and Vol. 16, No. 1, 1999). *This important book focuses on creating new ideas for using educational technologies such as the Internet, the World Wide Web and various software packages to further research and statistics. You will explore on-going debates relating to the theory of research, research methodology, and successful practices.* Information Technology in Educational Research and Statistics *also covers the debate on what statistical procedures are appropriate for what kinds of research designs.*

Educational Computing in the Schools: Technology, Communication, and Literacy, edited by Jay Blanchard, PhD (Vol. 15, No. 1, 1999). *Examines critical issues of technology, teaching, and learning in three areas: access, communication, and literacy. You will discover new ideas and practices for gaining access to and using technology in education from preschool through higher education.*

Logo: A Retrospective, edited by Cleborne D. Maddux, PhD, and D. LaMont Johnson, PhD (Vol. 14, No. 1/2, 1997). *"This book–honest and optimistic–is a must for those interested in any aspect of Logo: its history, the effects of its use, or its general role in education." (Dorothy M. Fitch, Logo consultant, writer, and editor, Derry, New Hampshire)*

Using Technology in the Classroom, edited by D. LaMont Johnson, PhD, Cleborne D. Maddux, PhD, and Leping Liu, MS (Vol. 13, No. 1/2, 1997). *"A guide to teaching with technology that emphasizes the advantages of transitioning from teacher-directed learning to learner-centered learning–a shift that can draw in even 'at-risk' kids." (Book News, Inc.)*

Multimedia and Megachange: New Roles for Educational Computing, edited by W. Michael Reed, PhD, John K. Burton, PhD, and Min Liu, EdD (Vol. 10, No. 1/2/3/4, 1995). *"Describes and analyzes issues and trends that might set research and development agenda for educators in the near future." (Sci Tech Book News)*

Language Minority Students and Computers, edited by Christian J. Faltis, PhD, and Robert A. DeVillar, PhD (Vol. 7, No. 1/2, 1990). *"Professionals in the field of language minority education, including ESL and bilingual education, will cheer this collection of articles written by highly respected, research writers, along with computer technologists, and classroom practitioners." (Journal of Computing in Teacher Education)*

Logo: Methods and Curriculum for Teachers, by Cleborne D. Maddux, PhD, and D. LaMont Johnson, PhD (Supp #3, 1989). *"An excellent introduction to this programming language for children." (Rena B. Lewis, Professor, College of Education, San Diego State University)*

Assessing the Impact of Computer-Based Instruction: A Review of Recent Research, by M. D. Roblyer, PhD, W. H. Castine, PhD, and F. J. King, PhD (Vol. 5, No. 3/4, 1988). *"A comprehensive and up-to-date review of the effects of computer applications on student achievement and attitudes." (Measurements & Control)*

Educational Computing and Problem Solving, edited by W. Michael Reed, PhD, and John K. Burton, PhD (Vol. 4, No. 3/4, 1988). *Here is everything that educators will need to know to use computers to improve higher level skills such as problem solving and critical thinking.*

The Computer in Reading and Language Arts, edited by Jay S. Blanchard, PhD, and George E. Mason, PhD (Vol. 4, No. 1, 1987). *"All of the [chapters] in this collection are useful, guiding the teacher unfamiliar with classroom computer use through a large number of available software options and classroom strategies." (Educational Technology)*

Computers in the Special Education Classroom, edited by D. LaMont Johnson, PhD, Cleborne D. Maddux, PhD, and Ann Candler, PhD (Vol. 3, No. 3/4, 1987). *"A good introduction to the use of computers in special education. . . . Excellent for those who need to become familiar with computer usage with special population students because they are contemplating it or because they have actually just begun to do it." (Science Books and Films)*

You Can Do It/Together, by Kathleen A. Smith, PhD, Cleborne D. Maddux, PhD, and D. LaMont Johnson, PhD (Supp #2, 1986). *A self-instructional textbook with an emphasis on the partnership system of learning that introduces the reader to four critical areas of computer technology.*

Computers and Teacher Training: A Practical Guide, by Dennis M. Adams, PhD (Supp #1, 1986). *"A very fine . . . introduction to computer applications in education." (International Reading Association)*

The Computer as an Educational Tool, edited by Henry F. Olds, Jr. (Vol. 3, No. 1, 1986). *"The category of tool uses for computers holds the greatest promise for learning, and this . . . book, compiled from the experiences of a good mix of practitioners and theorists, explains how and why." (Jack Turner, Technology Coordinator, Eugene School District 4-J, Oregon)*

Logo in the Schools, edited by Cleborne D. Maddux, PhD (Vol. 2, No. 2/3, 1985). *"An excellent blend of enthusiasm for the language of Logo mixed with empirical analysis of the language's effectiveness as a means of promoting educational goals. A much-needed book!" (Rena Lewis, PhD, Professor, College of Education, San Diego State University)*

Humanistic Perspectives on Computers in the Schools, edited by Steven Harlow, PhD (Vol. 1, No. 4, 1985). *"A wide spectrum of information." (Infochange)*

Distance Education:
What Works Well

Michael Corry, PhD
Chih-Hsiung Tu, PhD
Editors

Distance Education: What Works Well has been co-published simultaneously as *Computers in the Schools*, Volume 20, Number 3 2003.

The Haworth Press, Inc.

New York • London • Victoria (AU)
www.HaworthPress.com

Distance Education: What Works Well has been co-published simultaneously as *Computers in the Schools*, Volume 20, Number 3 2003.

Cover design by Lora Wiggins

Library of Congress Cataloging-in-Publication Data

Distance education : what works well / Michael Corry, Chih-Hsiung Tu, editors.
    p. cm.
    ISBN 0-7890-2287-7 (hard cover : alk. paper) – ISBN 0-7890-2288-5 (soft cover : alk. paper)
    1. Distance education–Computer-assisted instruction. 2. Educational technology. 3. World Wide Web. I. Corry, Michael. II. Tu, Chih-Hsiung.
LC5803.C65D553 2003
371.3'58–dc22
                                                                        2003017479

Indexing, Abstracting & Website/Internet Coverage

This section provides you with a list of major indexing & abstracting services. That is to say, each service began covering this periodical during the year noted in the right column. Most Websites which are listed below have indicated that they will either post, disseminate, compile, archive, cite or alert their own Website users with research-based content from this work. (This list is as current as the copyright date of this publication.)

Abstracting, Website/Indexing Coverage . . . . Year When Coverage Began

- *Academic Abstracts/CD-ROM* **1994**
- *Australian Education Index <www.acer.edu.au>* **2000**
- *Child Development Abstracts & Bibliography <www.ukans.edu>* . . . **2000**
- *CNPIEC Reference Guide: Chinese National Directory of Foreign Periodicals* **1995**
- *Computer Literature Index* **1993**
- *Computing Reviews* **1992**
- *Contents of this publication are indexed and abstracted in the ProQuest Education Complete database, available on ProQuest Information & Learning <www.proquest.com>* **1994**
- *Current Index to Journals in Education* **1991**
- *Education Abstracts. Published by The HW Wilson Company <www.hwwilson.com>* **1992**
- *Education Digest* **1991**
- *Education Index <www.hwwilson.com>* **1999**
- *Education Process Improvement Ctr, Inc. (EPICENTER) <www.epicent.com>* **2000**

(continued)

(continued)

*Exact start date to come.

Special Bibliographic Notes related to special journal issues (separates) and indexing/abstracting:

- indexing/abstracting services in this list will also cover material in any "separate" that is co-published simultaneously with Haworth's special thematic journal issue or DocuSerial. Indexing/abstracting usually covers material at the article/chapter level.
- monographic co-editions are intended for either non-subscribers or libraries which intend to purchase a second copy for their circulating collections.
- monographic co-editions are reported to all jobbers/wholesalers/approval plans. The source journal is listed as the "series" to assist the prevention of duplicate purchasing in the same manner utilized for books-in-series.
- to facilitate user/access services all indexing/abstracting services are encouraged to utilize the co-indexing entry note indicated at the bottom of the first page of each article/chapter/contribution.
- this is intended to assist a library user of any reference tool (whether print, electronic, online, or CD-ROM) to locate the monographic version if the library has purchased this version but not a subscription to the source journal.
- individual articles/chapters in any Haworth publication are also available through the Haworth Document Delivery Service (HDDS).

Distance Education: What Works Well

Contents

ABOUT THE EDITORS

Michael Corry, PhD, is Assistant Professor and Director of the Educational Technology Leadership Program at The George Washington University. Dr. Corry is intimately involved with course design and delivery as well as management of this pioneering program delivered via distance education at GWU. His research interests include distance learning theory and policy, faculty development, asynchronous learning, the integration of technology into K-12 and higher education settings, instructional design, and human-computer interaction. He is a principal investigator on two U.S. Department of Education grants focusing on preparing tomorrow's teachers to use technology. In addition to numerous publications and presentations relating to his research interests, Dr. Corry has designed and delivered faculty development workshops involving technology. Before coming to GWU, he taught at Indiana University as well as teaching high school in Utah and was an information systems consultant for Andersen Consulting.

Chih-Hsiung Tu, PhD, is Assistant Professor in the Educational Technology Leadership Program at The George Washington University. Dr. Tu was born in Taiwan, ROC, and appreciates the Chinese heritage of deep respect for education. His research interests include distance education, socio-cognitive learning, socio-cultural learning, social community learning, and knowledge management. He has numerous publications and presentations involving his research interests. Before coming to GWU, he taught at Arizona State University and in elementary schools in Taiwan, and served as Director of Library & Information Technology at Southwest College of Naturopathic Medicine in Tempe, Arizona.

INTRODUCTION

Michael Corry
Chih-Hsiung Tu

Distance Education:
What Works Well

In this publication you will find two types of articles. In the first half, articles describe real-life experiences in distance education. It begins with Wilhelmina Savenye and others describing the development of a digital high school from the early stages through "rookie camp" experiences. In a closely related article, Charalambos Vrasidas presents lessons learned in a virtual high school as well as practical recommendations on how to design successful online programs. In his article, J. Wanless Southwick discusses what has worked well and what hasn't worked well with distance education in the rural K-12 environment. Finally, Timothy R. Jenney and Eva K. Roupas describe the successes and failures of an innovative distance education project in 11 high schools and 5 middle schools.

MICHAEL CORRY is Assistant Professor, Department of Educational Leadership, Educational Technology Leadership Program, Graduate School of Education and Human Development, The George Washington University, Washington, DC 20052 (E-mail: mcorry@gwu.edu).
CHIH-HSIUNG TU is Assistant Professor, Department of Educational Leadership, Educational Technology Leadership Program, Graduate School of Education and Human Development, The George Washington University, Washington, DC 20052 (E-mail: ctu@gwu.edu).

[Haworth co-indexing entry note]: "Distance Education: What Works Well." Corry, Michael, and Chih-Hsiung Tu. Co-published simultaneously in *Computers in the Schools* (The Haworth Press, Inc.) Vol. 20, No. 3, 2003, pp. 1-2; and: *Distance Education: What Works Well* (ed: Michael Corry, and Chih-Hsiung Tu) The Haworth Press, Inc., 2003, pp. 1-2. Single or multiple copies of this article are available for a fee from The Haworth Document Delivery Service [1-800-HAWORTH, 9:00 a.m. - 5:00 p.m. (EST). E-mail address: docdelivery@haworthpress.com].

10.1300/J025v20n03_01

In the second half of this edition you will find practical advice on how to set up distance education so that you can take advantage of what works well. Marina Stock McIsaac and Elizabeth Harris Craft discuss how to train faculty to effectively use distance education. Chih-Hsiung Tu and Michael Corry build a case for the importance of interaction in a distance education classroom. They guide you through the steps of building active online communities. David Winograd provides practical advice on the roles, functions, and skills for moderators in online distance education. Atsusi Hirumi discusses the importance of teachers not getting overwhelmed with the time requirements associated with online distance education. He offers six tactics for optimizing time online. Finally, Ryan Watkins discusses decision-making issues regarding whether distance education is the right choice for you. He discusses the pros, cons, and requirements for successful distance education.

The final article in this edition differs somewhat from the other articles and is a thought provoking contribution by Cleborne D. Maddux. In his article, Dr. Maddux calls attention to some of the concerns and cautions that those involved in distance education need to be aware of.

Overall, we hope you find *Distance Education: What Works Well* to be filled with real-life experiences and practical advice involving what works well, what doesn't work well, and how to get to the point where most things work well. We look forward to future research and articles involving these important topics.

Wilhelmina Savenye
Herb Dwyer
Mary Niemczyk
Zane Olina
Alexander Kim
Adamos Nicolaou
Howard Kopp

Development of the Digital High School Project: A School-University Partnership

WILHELMINA SAVENYE is Associate Professor, Educational Technology, Division of Psychology in Education, Arizona State University, Tempe, AZ 85287-0611 (E-mail: savenye@asu.edu).
HERB DWYER is Coordinator of Advanced Projects, Instructional Systems and Technology, Tempe Union High School District, Tempe, AZ 85283 (E-mail: herbd@tuhsd.k12.az.us).
MARY NIEMCZYK is Faculty Associate, Aeronautical Management Technology, College of Technology and Applied Sciences, Arizona State University, Tempe, AZ 85212 (E-mail: niemczyk@asu.edu).
ZANE OLINA is Assistant Professor, Instructional Systems Program, Department of Educational Psychology and Learning Systems, Florida State University, Tallahassee, FL 32306-4453 (E-mail: olina@coe.fsu.edu).
ALEXANDER KIM is a graduate student, Learning and Instructional Technology, Arizona State University, Tempe, AZ 85287-0611 (E-mail: alexander.kim@asu.edu).
ADAMOS NICOLAOU is Teacher Trainer, Educational Technology Department, Cyprus Pedagogical Institute, Larnaca 6055, Cyprus (E-mail: adnicol@hotmail.com).
HOWARD KOPP is Instructional Technologist, Educational Technology, Arizona State University, Tempe, AZ 85287-0611.

[Haworth co-indexing entry note]: "Development of the Digital High School Project: A School-University Partnership." Savenye, Wilhelmina et al. Co-published simultaneously in *Computers in the Schools* (The Haworth Press, Inc.) Vol. 20, No. 3, 2003, pp. 3-14; and: *Distance Education: What Works Well* (ed: Michael Corry, and Chih-Hsiung Tu) The Haworth Press, Inc., 2003, pp. 3-14. Single or multiple copies of this article are available for a fee from The Haworth Document Delivery Service [1-800-HAWORTH, 9:00 a.m. - 5:00 p.m. (EST). E-mail address: docdelivery@haworthpress.com].

3

SUMMARY. A school district in the southwestern United States has over the past several years built its infrastructure to support high-quality technology integration by its teachers. The district partnered with a nearby university's educational technology graduate program to develop a digital high school project. Teachers and advanced instructional-design graduate students developed and field-tested four projects to aid teachers in implementing Web-based distance education, as follows: (1) A Rookie Camp was developed as an introductory unit to help students begin to use instruction delivered via WebCT courseware; (2) In *The Odyssey* Project a stand-alone Web-based courselet was developed for teachers to use to teach poetic devices and epic hero qualities related to *The Odyssey*; (3) A needs assessment yielded recommendations for teacher training and support for Web-based instruction; (4) Finally, a prototype unit was developed to help teachers learn about digital copyright issues related to distance learning via the Web. *[Article copies available for a fee from The Haworth Document Delivery Service: 1-800-HAWORTH. E-mail address: <docdelivery@haworthpress.com> Website: <http://www.HaworthPress.com> © 2003 by The Haworth Press, Inc. All rights reserved.]*

KEYWORDS. Preservice teacher education, technology integration, Web-based learning, distance education, partnerships, needs assessment, instructional development, educational technology, technology, teacher training

One high-school district in the Phoenix, Arizona, metropolitan area has, over the past seven years, built its infrastructure to support high-quality technology integration by its teachers. At one school, McClintock High School in Tempe, two staff members, Dr. Herb Dwyer and Mr. Bud Boyle (Dwyer & Boyle, 1999), had, over these years, explored various scenarios to meet the challenge of improving student success using educational technology. They and other teachers determined that many types of students could benefit from nontraditional delivery of instructional materials. Such students might include: "turnaround students," those taking classes for more than one time due to failure; homebound youth; students who had earlier dropped out of school; accelerated students and those interested in less-common electives; and students outside the school, such as charter school and home-schooled students. At McClintock High the technology coordinator, administrators, and several innovative teachers determined that the time had come to take advantage of what technology could now do for their teachers and students. They knew their school was ready to take the next step toward true technology integration.

The school personnel saw this next step as consisting of developing several levels of Web-based and Web-supplemented instructional materials and programs. At one level, they partnered with the Virtual High School (VHS) out of Concord, Massachusetts, to secure access to advanced placement courses for students who could not otherwise take these courses. One teacher enrolled in the VHS's teacher-training program. During the first year, five McClintock students were able to take such courses as Advanced International Politics and Advanced Microbiology, all fully Web-based courses. At another level, one teacher, Mrs. Karen Crane, set out to develop Web-supplemented materials, such as WebQuests, for her lower-level English students. She found that students' interest in these innovative materials seemed to decrease the dropout rate in her course. At another level, it was hoped that teachers could develop Web-based "courselets" for many content areas that students who could not attend school (e.g., due to illness or suspension) could complete on their own. The school also plans to develop Web-based instruction to help students prepare for state-mandated exams (Dwyer & Boyle, 1999).

The overall goals of the initial plans were to increase access to instruction through these various means, and also to decrease instructional costs. During the strategic planning, the district evaluated several Web course authoring programs and selected WebCT for its major systems, although teachers also have access to other software.

The district had recently passed a bond issue to fund purchases of computer hardware and software, along with significant upgrades of the district's technology infrastructure; however, here, as elsewhere in our public schools, there is little to no funding for teacher training, student and faculty support, and development of materials.

THE COLLABORATIVE PARTNERSHIP

Meanwhile, during the spring of 2000, at a nearby university, a faculty member from an educational technology graduate program sought "real-world" projects for students in her advanced instructional development class. A fortunately-timed call to the technology coordinator at the high school (not coincidentally, an alumnus of our doctoral program) seeded the beginning of a collaborative school-university partnership that has added to the nucleus of the Web-based school project.

Initially, the school district and university personnel identified several needs that they hoped could be answered through the partnership. The school district wanted to add a scholarly focus to their technology efforts. They also hoped the graduate students would provide the teachers and staff with an instructional design perspective, to complement the desired exemplary use of technology skills. It was hoped that, in addition to the extra resources the university program would provide, the educational technology graduate students and professor would bring the school and the district a fresh and different perspective.

The university professor and graduate students, of course, desired to fill their need for advanced real-world instructional design projects, as well as a proving ground to learn more about school needs and applications of technology. Not incidentally, the school district surrounds the university, and this close proximity aided all in staying in close touch.

Finally, the university professor and the school technology director wished that the personal relationships that developed as a result of the partnership would sow the seeds for future collaborative projects to benefit students and faculty in the school district and university.

DEVELOPMENT OF THE PROJECT

During the spring of 2000, five students in the advanced instructional development course at the university learned about principles of Web-based development and course delivery and techniques for conducting needs assessments. For instance, they learned some of the basic principles of distance learning, especially Web-based distance learning (cf. Kahn, 1997; McIsaac & Gunawardena, 1996; Moore & Kearsley, 1996). They discussed how to determine if a course is suitable for Web delivery by learning the principles of Porter (1997). They learned about qualities of instructors who are more successful in developing innovative Internet-based programs (cf. Beaudoin, 1990; Collis, 1996; Gunawardena, 1992; Muffaletto, 1997). They also learned about aspects of learner expectations in distance instruction (cf. Moore, 1989).

The focus of the course then shifted to developing projects. The five students discussed advanced instructional design techniques, particularly instructional strategies, based on the work of Smith and Ragan (1999). They also learned how to implement sound instructional design principles in Web-based environments (cf. Eastmond & Zieghan, 1995; Hirumi & Bermudez, 1996; Ritchie & Hoffman, 1996). They learned about some of the issues facing teachers and students who use the computer-mediated communications that such systems as WebCT allow (cf. Bull, Bull, & Sigmon, 1997; Lewis, Whitaker & Julian, 1995). Students were reminded of the importance of good visual design in Web development (cf. Grabinger, 1989). Finally, after students developed their projects, they field-tested them according to the principles of Dick, Carey, and Carey (2001).

Four projects were completed, all developed in partnership with teachers, technology coordinators, and students. These projects are presented in the discussion that follows.

ROOKIE CAMP:
AN INTRODUCTORY UNIT FOR WEB-SUPPLEMENTED
INSTRUCTION AT THE HIGH SCHOOL LEVEL

Introducing and successfully implementing Web-based courses can be difficult. Many obstacles may present themselves. Difficulties may lie not only in securing agreement from administration and faculty, but also in aiding students in becoming successful in these new environments.

Ease of use is critical to promoting student success in computer-assisted instruction and distance education. If students continually need help in overcoming obstacles in the software, they will become frustrated quickly (Heinich, Molenda, Russell, & Smaldino, 1999). Although it is probably true that many high school students have some computer experience, relatively few have had exposure to using the Web as part of their classroom instruction. In order to insure success, learners need to be ready to work with this new tool. Learner readiness involves gaining competencies in using navigation tools and becoming familiar with the learning environment (Twigg, 1999; Winiecki, 1999).

In addition to becoming familiar with using the computer to learn in new ways, student success is also based on using successful study skills and learning strategies. Students participating in distance education courses have stated that improving study skills is a key element in their success (Visser & Visser, 2000). The skills that students need in order to succeed in all forms of instruction, especially individual instruction, play an important role in effective distance education as well. Some of these skills include planning and organizing for learning, and learning to apply skills developed in the classroom or a paper-and-pencil environment to complete computer-assisted instruction (Cates, 1991).

The high school selected WebCT as the courseware most teachers would use to develop Web-supplemented instruction. In order to ease the transition to Web-supplemented courses and to promote student success, the "Rookie Camp" unit in WebCT was developed. The Rookie Camp unit provides students with an introduction to the elements they will be working with in a Web-supplemented learning environment (Niemczyk, 2000). It was planned that the unit would become a "default tool" to be included in all WebCT courses at this high school. Rookie Camp would be the first unit the high school students in Web-supplemented courses would complete.

In developing Rookie Camp the developer conducted a needs assessment to determine what should be included in the unit. She then developed design specifications for the school staff to review. After securing their input, she wrote a flowchart and storyboards from which to develop the prototype unit. The prototype unit begins with an introduction that informs students of the unit objectives. Students next learn about the course home page, which depicts nine icons. Each of the nine icons and the course management tools they represent are then explained in detail. After the students work through the Rookie Camp course content, they are provided with practice activities, a review, and a quiz. In addition, the developer provided a job aid, or reference sheet, that explains WebCT terminology along with study skills reminders for students. This job aid may also be provided to parents, along with suggestions for how they can help their children successfully use the Web for course work.

Students in a freshman English class at the high school participated in a formative evaluation of the Rookie Camp unit. They worked through the unit and then completed the quiz and an attitude survey. The findings from this evaluation will be used to improve the next version of Rookie Camp. One result of the project is that a second unit for Rookie Camp is planned; that is, a unit that will provide students with more suggestions on how to be successful learners in this environment. That second unit could also include various links pointing to learning tool Web sites and resources (Niemczyk, Dwyer, & Savenye, 2000).

POETIC DEVICES AND THE EPIC HERO
IN *THE ODYSSEY* OF HOMER:
THE ODYSSEY PROJECT

Two graduate students (Kim & Nicolaou, 2000) and their teacher partner, Ms. Erin Kahn, developed a Web-based unit to help teachers teach *The Odyssey*. Other additional purposes of the project were to provide teachers with a concrete model of a stand-alone, Web-based "courselet," to introduce teachers to instructional design principles and processes, and to help teachers become familiar with the principles of Web-based instruction. The project was designed to be used both as a stand-alone unit and a supplemental unit of instruction, either synchronously or asynchronously. It was also designed to meet teachers' needs, as well as the school partner's need for creating a working model and template of what a Web-based course should look like.

The developers initially worked with the teacher to select a topic for the model unit that many teachers could easily incorporate into different subject areas. Together the team then identified the content to be covered and developed the unit objectives.

The unit teaches students how to identify several poetic devices and epic hero qualities in given passages. Students work through information about each objective and then complete interactive practice. They receive specific feedback about each of their answers. At the end of the unit, students complete a quiz. The unit also allows students to explore an interactive map of Greece and the Mediterranean region, with references to events in *The Odyssey*.

The project was developed over a period of several weeks and was used and evaluated at the end of the partner teacher's spring semester. The project was field-tested with eight ninth-grade English students. Students answered multiple-choice items on a quiz Web page, and then submitted their answers electronically to the designers. The courselet concluded with an online student attitude survey consisting of five-choice Likert-type questions and several open-ended questions.

Students' attitudes were very favorable. They reported that they enjoyed using the courselet and would use more Web-based instructional materials like *The Odyssey* unit. Teachers' attitudes were also positive. Student achievement, however, was rather poor. This may have been influenced by the fact that, unfortunately, field-testing had occurred at the same time as statewide testing.

Future plans include a revision to include more descriptive feedback and more short activities sections to give students additional opportunities to practice what they have learned. More graphics will be added to the instruction as well. The most important lessons learned from this project were (a) the importance of frequent and regular face-to-face teacher-designer meetings, and (b) that time management is critical.

A NEEDS ASSESSMENT FOR TEACHER TRAINING AND SUPPORT

One doctoral student conducted a study to determine how the district could best train and support teachers in using Web-based instruction. In her needs assessment study, she surveyed the literature, researched case studies on the Web, and conducted structured interviews and surveys with school district technology coordinators and teachers (Olina, 2000).

Olina found that the major missing component in most technology-integration projects in schools has been the lack of adequate teacher training and support (U.S. Office of Technology Assessment, 1995; President's Committee of Advisors on Science and Technology, 1997). Based on her preliminary work with the school district personnel, Olina determined that she would develop a "white paper" that would further inform the decision-making process regarding the implementation of Web-based and Web-supplemented instruction at the high school and across the district.

In her review, Olina found many common barriers to technology integration in teaching. Among these barriers were the increased preparation time necessary and a lack of (a) awareness about the general benefits of distance education, (b) faculty compensation and incentives, and (c) access to appropriate technologies. Other hindrances included a lack of shared vision for distance education in the organization, institutional barriers, and lack of support staff to help develop courses (Moore & Kearsley, 1996; U.S. Office of Technology Assessment, 1995). Lack of time appeared to be the single major factor hindering technology integration. Providing teachers with help in designing their courses, providing them with extra time to modify their current classroom instructional practices, identifying incentives for technology integration in the classroom, and recognizing faculty intellectual property rights are a few of the strategies that would help instructors overcome these barriers.

When designing teacher training for Web-based or Web-supplemented instruction, special attention should be paid both to the content and format of such training. Teachers should be introduced to two distinct features of online pedagogy. First, the teaching paradigm must change from the traditional lecture format to one more suitable for online instruction. Secondly, teachers need to learn the skills and strategies for facilitating effective online interaction (The University of Illinois Faculty Seminar Report, 1999). Most importantly, teacher training should focus on the use of technology in teaching rather than the acquisition of skills using software (U. S. Office of Technology Assessment, 1995; President's Committee of Advisors on Science and Technology, 1997). A variety of approaches, such as developing technology-rich classrooms as demonstration sites, providing teachers with first-hand distance education experiences, training master teachers who then serve as resources to their colleagues, and providing access to technical support staff, could be used in combination to address the varied needs of educators.

However, unless a systemic approach to technology integration is adopted, individual teacher training initiatives are likely to be ineffective (Olina, 2000). Developing a clear vision for technology integration that is directly linked to improvement of classroom practice and is shared by instructors, administrators, and technology support staff alike is the first step toward successful technology integration. Ensuring access to adequate technology in the classrooms both by teachers and students, along with high-quality technical support, and allocating adequate financial resources for teacher professional development should become core components of such a vision (Olina, Dwyer, & Savenye, 2000).

DIGITAL COPYRIGHT FOR TEACHERS

The final project developed as part of the partnership concerned with helping teachers learn about copyright issues related to Web development. Kopp (2000) developed a prototype design for a Web-based self-instructional unit to help teachers learn about copyright issues in the digital age. As part of this unit, teachers learn how to identify material that can be copyrighted, how to secure copyright permission, and how to follow guidelines of educational use of copyrighted material. The prototype materials have been field-tested with teachers and are currently being revised for dissemination.

CONCLUSION

This one-semester collaborative project between a school and university was pronounced a success by all parties. The five educational technology graduate students and their school partners completed four projects, each of which would impact the high school as well as the district. Niemczyk's Rookie Camp unit formed the prototype for the first unit that students will use when they begin courses or supplemental materials that are delivered using WebCT. Elements of the Rookie Camp project also have informed the district's decision to build a template to make it easier for teachers to build WebCT materials. An adapted version of Nicolaou and Kim's *The Odyssey* project will soon be available on the Web for teachers in various content areas, especially language arts, but also history and social studies, to use in teaching their courses. Olina's white paper on teacher training and support was shared with the school superintendent, as well as many other teachers and administrators, and has informed the high school district's plans for helping teachers better integrate distance education and Web technology into classroom learning. Kopp's design for a Web-based unit about digital copyright has been successfully used by teachers and staff in the high school.

IMPLICATIONS FOR THE FUTURE

In developing our partnership we learned many lessons. Among them is the importance of building partnerships based on people, rather than institutions. We found it advantageous to build an informal rather than formal partnership, and thereby enjoy the flexibility this has offered. While we worked hard to meet the needs of all parties in our partnership, in the future we plan to do even better in helping our university students and teachers communicate early, more frequently, and more clearly as they work. We plan to offer our graduate students more concrete skills in how to more rapidly gather and use data during the needs assessment phases of their projects, and hold more discussions about relationship-building as they work. Of course, we continue to learn that success in such projects, where often most work is voluntarily done, builds over time.

Our collaboration formed the foundation for both extensions of these four original projects and for new ones. In particular, the plan to develop *The Odyssey* project as a model for helping teachers learn about the possibilities of Web-based and distance instruction is being realized. One of the pioneer Web technology teachers in the high school, Mrs. Karen Crane, and Dr. Herb Dwyer, now Coordinator of Advanced Projects for the district, subsequently partnered with a graduate student who did her internship with the high school. Christine Ziobrowski and Mrs. Crane designed computer-based instruction for the school's Independent Learning Center. Students who may have missed or must redo lessons go to the center to complete their work. Several students typically work on different lessons in the center at any one time, with just one or two teachers to help them. This has led the school and the team to determine that partially self-paced units, and self-guided units will benefit students. The new instructional unit builds on and extends *The Odyssey* project, helping 9th-to 12th-grade students in understanding this literary work.

Other aspects of our collaboration have included offering opportunities for beginning instructional design graduate students to develop instructional units with teachers at the high school. More advanced students in distance education classes may also work with school teachers and staff to build new Web-based supplements and to conduct distance education research related to the needs of K-12 education. Other graduate students have completed internships with the district in the area of teacher training for technology. We are also now in the process of collaborating to secure funding for other projects to enhance student learning through technology.

Our collaboration has given us a chance to apply the ideas we have encountered in the research and development literature in distance education. However, the school district and university partners agree that the time is ripe for bold initiatives, going beyond what has been done in the past, essentially beyond what may have become our "comfort zone." We plan to explore, for instance, developing more open-ended learning environments with no ceiling in terms of what students can accomplish. We continue to struggle with how to "chunk" Web-based instruction to accommodate a wide variety of student skill levels. We are also conducting research on how to deliver multimedia lessons and courses over the Web to aid teachers in using a wide range of applications of technology for the classroom.

With the explosive growth of the Internet, many schools and universities are turning to the Internet to both supplement traditional course materials with Web-supported materials and courses, and to deliver fully Web-based courses. We believe collaborations among organizations like ours hold great promise for building and developmentally testing high-quality learning materials for students and support for teachers. We plan to continue to explore Web-based technologies for helping students learn and to look for increasingly innovative ways to partner.

REFERENCES

Beaudoin, M. (1990). The instructor's changing role in distance education. *The American Journal of Distance Education*, *4*(2), 21-29.

Bull, G., Bull, G., & Sigmon, T. (September, 1997). Common protocols for shared communities. *Learning and Leading with Technology*, *25*(1), 50-53.

Cates, W. M. (1991). What we need to teach students *before* they work on computer-assisted instruction: Lessons gleaned from CAI failures. *International Journal of Instructional Media*, *18*(2), 129-140.

Collis, B. (1996). *Tele-learning in a digital world–the future of distance learning.* Boston, MA: International Thompson Computer Press.

Dick, W., Carey, L., & Carey, J. (2001). *The systematic design of instruction* (5th ed.). New York: Longman.

Dwyer, H., & Boyle, B. (1999). *Web-based instruction at McClintock High School: A report on the current status of the Web-based education project developed at McClintock High School.* Tempe, AZ: Tempe Unified High School District.

Eastmond, D., & Ziegahn, L. (1995). Instructional design for the online classroom. In A. Berge & M. Collins (Eds.), *Computer mediated communication and the online classroom* (Vol. 3, pp. 59-80). Creskill, NJ: Hampton Press.

Grabinger, R. S. (1989). Screen layout design: Research into the overall appearance on the screen. *Computers in Human Behavior, 3,* 173-183.

Gunawardena, C. N. (1992). Changing faculty roles for audiographics and online teaching. *The American Journal of Distance Education, 6*(3), 58-71.

Heinich, R., Molenda, M., Russell, J. D., & Smaldino, S. (1999). *Instructional media and technologies for learning* (6th ed.). Upper Saddle River, NJ: Merrill, an imprint of Prentice-Hall.

Hirumi, A., & Bermudez, A. (1996). Interactivity, distance education and instructional systems design converge on the information superhighway. *Journal of Research on Computing in Education, 29*(1), 1-16.

Khan, B. H. (Ed.). (1997). *Web-based instruction.* Englewood Cliffs, NJ: Educational Technology Publications.

Kim, A., & Nicolaou, A. (2000). *Poetic devices and the epic hero in* The Odyssey *of Homer.* Tempe, AZ: McClintock High School.

Kopp, H. (2000). *Digital copyright for teachers.* Tempe, AZ: McClintock High School.

Lewis, J., Whitaker, J., & Julian, J. (1995). Distance education for the 21st century: The future of national and international telecomputing networks in distance education. In Z. Berge & M. Collins (Eds.), *Computer mediated communication and the online classroom* (Vol. 3, pp. 13-30). Creskill, NJ: Hampton Press.

McIsaac, M. S., & Gunawardena, C. N. (1996). Distance education. In D. H. Jonassen (Ed.), *Handbook of research for educational communications and technology* (pp. 403-437). New York: Simon & Schuster McMillan.

Moore, M. G. (1989). Distance education: A learner's system. *Lifelong Learning: An Omnibus of Practice and Research, 12*(8), 8-11.

Moore, M., & Kearsley, G. (1996). *Distance education: A systems view.* Belmont, CA: Wadsworth.

Muffoletto, R. (1997, March). Reflections on designing and producing an Internet-based course. *TechTrends, 42*(2), 50-53.

Niemczyk, M. (2000). *Rookie camp.* Tempe, AZ: McClintock High School.

Niemczyk, M., Dwyer, H., & Savenye, W. (2000, October 25-28). *Rookie camp: An introductory unit for Web-supplemented instruction at the high-school level.* Paper presented at the national conference of the Association of Educational Communications and Technology, Denver, CO.

Olina, Z. (2000). *Recommendations for teacher training and support systems for Web-supplemented and Web-based instruction in Tempe High School District.* Tempe, AZ: McClintock High School.

Olina, Z., Dwyer, H, & Savenye, W. (2000, October 25-28). *Support and training for faculty who will teach using the Web.* Paper presented at the national conference of the Association of Educational Communications and Technology, Denver, CO.

President's Committee of Advisors on Science and Technology. (1997, March). *Panel on educational technology report to the president on the use of technology to strengthen K-12 education in the United States.* [Online]. Retrieved April 8, 2000, from http://www.whitehouse.gov/WH/EOP/OSTP/NSTC/PCAST/k-12ed.html#5.t

Porter, L. A. (1997). *Creating the virtual classroom–distance learning with the Internet.* New York: Wiley.

Ritchie, D. C., & Hoffman, R. (1996). Using instructional design principles to amplify learning on the World Wide Web. In B. Rubin, J. D. Price, J. Willis & D. A. Willis (Eds.), *Teaching and teacher education annual, 1996* (pp. 813-815). Charlottesville, VA: Association for the Advancement of Computing in Education. [ERIC Document Reproduction Service No. ED415835.]

Smith, P. J., & Ragan, T. J. (1999). Conditions-based models for designing instruction. In D. H. Jonassen (Ed.), *Handbook of research for educational communications and technology* (pp. 541-569). New York: Simon & Schuster McMillan.

Twigg, C. (1999). *Improving learning and reducing costs: Redesigning large-enrollment courses.* [Online]. Retrieved January 24, 2002, from http://www.center.rpi.edu/PewSym/mono1.html

University of Illinois. (1999). *Teaching at an Internet distance: The pedagogy of online teaching and learning (The report of a 1998-1999 University of Illinois faculty seminar).* [Online]. Retrieved January 24, 2002, from http://www.vpaa.uillinois.edu/tid/

U.S. Office of Technology Assessment. (1995, March 31). *Teachers and technology: Making the connection.* (OTA-EHR-616. GPO stock #052-003-01409-2). [Online]. Retrieved January 24, 2002, from http://www.wws.princeton.edu/~ota/ns20/alpha_f.html

Visser, L, & Visser, Y. (2000, February). *Integrated cognitive and affective student support in distance education.* Paper presented at the national conference of the Association for Educational Communications and Technology, Long Beach, CA.

Winiecki, D. J. (1999, August). Preparing students for asynchronous computer-mediated coursework: Design and delivery of a "distance education bootcamp." *Proceedings of the 15th annual conference on distance learning and teaching,* pp. 433-437. Madison, WI.

Charalambos Vrasidas

The Design, Development, and Implementation of LUDA Virtual High School

SUMMARY. The purpose of this paper is to present the Large Unit District Association virtual high school (LUDA-VHS) project and discuss its design, development, and implementation. A model developed at the Center for the Application of Information Technologies for designing online classes will be presented and discussed. The focus of the paper will be to present the lessons learned and provide practical recommendations on how to design successful online programs. Issues to be discussed include the following: recruiting, training, and compensating teachers; selecting and supporting students; developing instructional strategies for online learning; building a sense of community; educating the public on the benefits of online education; providing equal access; building quality assurance mechanisms. *[Article copies available for a fee from The Haworth Document Delivery Service: 1-800-HAWORTH. E-mail address: <docdelivery@haworthpress.com> Website: <http://www.HaworthPress.com> © 2003 by The Haworth Press, Inc. All rights reserved.]*

KEYWORDS. Virtual high school, distance education, distributed learning, educational technology, evaluation

CHARALAMBOS VRASIDAS is Coordinator of Research and Evaluation, Center for the Application of Information Technology, Western Illinois University, Macomb, IL 61455 (E-mail: cvrasidas@cait.org).

[Haworth co-indexing entry note]: "The Design, Development, and Implementation of LUDA Virtual High School." Vrasidas, Charalambos. Co-published simultaneously in *Computers in the Schools* (The Haworth Press, Inc.) Vol. 20, No. 3, 2003, pp. 15-25; and: *Distance Education: What Works Well* (ed: Michael Corry, and Chih-Hsiung Tu) The Haworth Press, Inc., 2003, pp. 15-25. Single or multiple copies of this article are available for a fee from The Haworth Document Delivery Service [1-800-HAWORTH, 9:00 a.m. - 5:00 p.m. (EST). E-mail address: docdelivery@haworthpress.com].

http://www.haworthpress.com/store/product.asp?sku=J025
© 2003 by The Haworth Press, Inc. All rights reserved.
10.1300/J025v20n03_03

Information and communication technologies have a major impact on education and training around the world. Technology can improve access to education and provide time flexibility for learners by creating both synchronous and asynchronous learning environments (Berge & Collins, 1995; Mason, 1994; Owston, 1997; Vrasidas & McIsaac, 2000). Distance education (DE) as a field has grown from simple correspondence education to a highly sophisticated, distributed interactive learning experience (Vrasidas & Glass, 2002). Internet access in U.S. public schools is growing rapidly. According to the National Center of Education Statistics (2000), by the fall of 2000, 98% of public schools in the United States had access to the Internet, in comparison to 35% of public schools that had access to the Internet in 1994. Furthermore, the ratio of students to instructional computers in public schools had decreased to 5 to 1, which is the ratio that is considered as the appropriate ratio for effective use of computers in schools. As computers and the Internet invade public schools, opportunities for DE grow.

One of the trends in DE is the development of virtual high schools. Virtual high schools (VHS) are offering alternative solutions to educate populations of students who are not well served otherwise. Despite the criticism and skepticism over DE efforts, DE classes and VHS are growing. For example, the Virtual High School, a consortium of high schools offering online courses taught by consortium teachers for students in participating schools, during the academic year 2000-2001, offered more than 200 high school courses to nearly 4,000 students in 350 schools in 30 states (Kozma et al., 2000).

DESCRIPTION OF LUDA-VHS

Technology is blurring the boundaries between traditional face-to-face and DE, and educators need to revisit their fundamental assumptions about teaching and learning (Vrasidas & McIsaac, 1999). Students no longer need to sit in a room with desks in rows for learning to occur. LUDA-VHS is based on the assumption that learning occurs when the student is given opportunities for interaction with the content, the teacher, other students, and tools.

LUDA-VHS Overview

LUDA-VHS is an effort by the LUDA Education Foundation (a nonprofit organization) in partnership with the Center for the Application of Information Technologies (CAIT) at Western Illinois University to provide opportunities for DE to high school students. LUDA-VHS has as a major goal to use technology for developing alternative ways for serving the needs of school districts and providing quality education to high school students in Illinois. LUDA districts serve more than 50% of all high school students in the state.

The LUDA Education Foundation appointed the LUDA-VHS planning committee, which consisted of members of the LUDA Education Foundation, CAIT personnel, and representatives from LUDA school districts. The planning committee's major role was to work closely with three teachers from three different Illinois schools districts and CAIT personnel for the design, development, and implementation of a pilot online class. The goals for the pilot class were to help:

1. resolve the technical, administrative, developmental, and implementation issues relating to online class development;
2. identify a process for online class development; and
3. identify the lessons learned from this pilot so they can be used for the development of more courses.

The first class developed was Consumer Education, a required class for graduation in the state of Illinois. The class was launched in June 2001 at the three schools where the teachers who developed the content were working full time. The class lasted for six weeks. The project was funded in part by CAIT for an approximate development cost of $150,000. Additional teacher substitutes, traveling expenses, and extra hours spent on the project were covered by the respective school districts involved in the development of the summer class. K-12 projects developed at CAIT are funded in part by the Illinois Board of Higher Education.

Student Web Site

Students used their assigned user ID and password to log in to the Consumer Education Web site using an Internet browser such as Internet Explorer or Netscape. From their Internet browser students accessed the class material, activities, discussions, and homework. They were able to submit their work via a browser, communicate with their peers and teacher, participate in online discussions, view their grades, and receive feedback. In addition, there was a printed class manual that included the procedures, policies, activities, netiquette, time management tips, and general guidelines on how to successfully complete the class. The content of the class and lessons was structured in a sequential manner. Students could not move forward to the next lesson until they completed all of the activities in each of the previous lessons. The student's online gradebook was connected to the class Web site, and it kept track of the activities and lessons students completed.

Teachers' Lounge

In addition to the student Web site, the teacher had access to another Web site called the "Teachers' Lounge." Teachers accessed that Web site with their user ID and password. There, they could create a class, assign students, view the students' submitted activities, maintain student records, and assign grades that the students could view from the student Web site. In addition, they could use the e-mail function of the site to send feedback to individual students, multiple students, or all students. Furthermore, the teacher could sort data in the gradebook using various criteria and generate reports for printing or e-mailing to parents.

Course Development Process

Three LUDA teachers worked closely with the project manager and two instructional designers from CAIT to develop the content for the Consumer Education class. During the first meeting, instructional designers gave an overview of the process for developing online classes and discussed several ideas for providing interaction in online environments. In order to facilitate content preparation by the teachers, a template was given to teachers, which was used by CAIT designers for other DE courses. This template provides a basic structure of how to organize the content for an online class and to structure its goals, objectives, activities, communication strategies, and interaction. During the meeting, teachers were assigned units of content they felt more comfortable developing. Following the first meeting, teachers worked on their own to develop a sample lesson from the content they were assigned. They sent that lesson via e-mail to CAIT designers who provided feedback. Following that, there were periodic meetings among teachers and CAIT designers during which the status of the project was discussed and feedback was provided on content development and on the class Web site. After class content was developed, teachers were trained in teaching online and in using the class tools and Web site.

Student Selection

Students were selected with the help of guidance counselors and teachers in the three schools. First, an announcement was made in the three schools that Consumer Education was to be offered online. Students were invited to apply for a place in the online class roster. Applications were accompanied by parental consent as well as by the student's counselor or another teacher's consent who could comment on the student's self-motivation, writing skills, communication skills, computer skills, and work habits. The maximum number of students for each class was set to 20.

Evaluation

Thorough evaluations of DE efforts are essential for the success and growth of the field. The LUDA-VHS evaluation was authorized by the LUDA Education Foundation and was designed and carried out by CAIT's Research and Evaluation Unit. The data for the evaluation were based on detailed memos and notes from meetings of the planning committee, production meetings, teacher workshops, teacher interviews and focus discussions, surveys completed by students, and face-to-face and phone interviews with principals, superintendents, and other school staff from the three participating school districts.

A general feeling among all stakeholders was that the project met its goals, and all stakeholders were satisfied with the results of the pilot class delivered during the summer. A good indicator of the project's success is the fact that all stakeholders interviewed indicated a high level of satisfaction with the project. The class content and materials were of high quality and rigor. Teachers were satisfied with their students' ability to troubleshoot, engage in the class activities and lessons, meet deadlines, work independently, and ask for help when needed. Students gave high ratings to the class and were pleased with the level of interaction with their teacher. Students felt that their teachers communicated regularly and a timely manner with them. The majority of students agreed that they learned a lot of information about consumer issues, and they would recommend this class to their peers.

A combination of factors influenced project success. The project was successful because a synergy of people, resources, and processes worked together in a team spirit, sharing the same vision. Alignment between the goals of the project with the LUDA strategic plan, as well as with the participant schools' technology plans, also contributed to the project's success. CAIT's experience in distance learning, commitment to the project, and timely technical support provided during class deployment were also important factors. An additional factor was the strong sense of ownership and commitment to the project by the participating schools. School districts that participated in the pilot were involved in the development of the class. Teachers who developed the content were who taught the class in the summer, and they put their best effort forward in making the project a success.

Although the project was successful, there are several issues that need to be addressed to ensure that the project continues to succeed and serve the needs of LUDA districts and their students. The following summary of issues and recommendations may be very helpful for other schools interested in developing VHS projects.

LESSONS LEARNED

Course Development Process

One of the goals of the LUDA-VHS pilot project was to establish a model to be used for the development and implementation of DE classes. The results of this evaluation indicated that the model used for developing the summer pilot class could serve as the basis for the development of additional courses. One thing that should be revised is the number of teachers involved in content development. It would be more practical to work with two teachers for developing content. Even though three teachers provided multiple voices and ideas for class content and activities, working with three teachers and coordinating content development was not very efficient.

Another issue in course development was time. The results of the project evaluation indicated that the short time frame of the project caused complications in the development and deployment of the class. This class was developed in a period of four months, and content development was not completed until a week before class was launched. For future development efforts, class production (including content, manuals, and Web site) should be allotted eight to twelve months. Class production should be completed at least two months ahead of launching day, which will allow enough time for usability testing, tryouts, and technology and content revisions.

In order to avoid some of the complications that emerged in the development and deployment of the summer pilot class, in addition to Web designers and graphic artists, four key staff members are needed for future classes. Their titles and duties are briefly outlined below:

1. Project manager
    a. In charge of the project, coordinates the efforts of all persons involved and assigns or reassigns duties according to resources, personnel, skills, and timelines.
    b. Establishes the timeline in collaboration with LUDA Education Foundation and monitors project progress.
2. Content coordinator
    a. In charge of collecting the content from teachers, ensures they follow the template, coordinates the communication among teachers and design team.
3. Technology coordinator
    a. Must be involved from the beginning stages of the project to map out the technology needs, raise possible issues and known problems with certain technologies, etc.
    b. In charge of all technology components of the class, including servers, software, database applications, network issues, etc.
4. Instructional designer
    a. Provides training to teachers on how to develop and teach online classes.
    b. Responsible for all the instruction, activities, assessment, layout, interface design, and navigation.
    c. Conducts usability testing with the help of the technology coordinator.

Content, Pedagogy, and Structure

Students in Consumer Education had to complete all activities and lessons in a sequential manner. This had an impact on their work because if they could not complete an activity, they had to wait until they received feedback from the teacher before moving on. Based on evaluation findings, two major revisions were incorporated in the class. First, the architecture of the class Web site was opened up thus allowing students to complete any lesson in any sequence under teacher guidance. This gives teachers the freedom to choose lessons and activities they feel necessary and which match their personal teaching philosophy and school's needs. In addition, if students need help completing an activity, they can continue working on other activities and lessons until they receive feedback from the teacher.

The second major revision was the implementation of a collaborative project that is expected to increase the amount of interaction among students (Vrasidas & McIsaac, 1999; Vrasidas, 2000). It has been argued that one of the most neglected variables in education is learner-learner interaction (Johnson, 1981). During the summer, the online learner-learner interaction that took place was in the discussion area, where students logged on to discuss the teacher-developed questions. For the fall of 2001, a collaborative project was incorporated which required students to collaborate to rent an apartment. To successfully complete the group project, students needed to collaborate, search online for information, collect data, share results, and negotiate the best deal possible.

One of the strengths of the online environment is that it allows for interactions at multiple levels. In addition to promoting learner-learner and learner-teacher interactions, LUDA-VHS should consider the possibility of allowing outsiders with experience in the content of the class to participate in discussions with the students. For example, a banker could be given access to the class discussion board in the role of guest lecturer and answer questions from students that relate to the banker's expertise. A real-estate agent could collaborate with a group of students and help them identify the best apartment to meet their needs and goals. Furthermore, subsequent courses could allow students to identify the discussion questions and collaborate with peers to moderate online discussions and summarize results.

What seems to be missing from the summer pilot class is the sense of community among students. As LUDA-VHS expands, the Internet should be used to bring together students from different school districts in a shared Web space where they can chat, discuss ideas for projects, and organize debates and competitions. Activities that will require the participation of multiple schools and students need to be planned carefully, but they are essential if LUDA-VHS will grow to become a viable way for LUDA schools to educate children with community ideals.

Equity and the Digital Divide

One of the missions of LUDA-VHS should be to equally serve the needs of students regardless of socioeconomic status, ethnicity, and gender. The LUDA Education Foundation, in collaboration with respective school districts, should establish policies to ensure equal access to classes offered by LUDA-VHS. One such policy could be the establishment of scholarships and awards for low-income students. A laptop program could be established with the partnership of large corporations and Internet providers who might be willing to participate in the project. Schools could lend students laptops for a semester, so they could complete an online class. Once the class is completed, the student would return the laptop to the school, so that other students could use it in subsequent semesters.

Student Recruitment and Preparation

In order for LUDA-VHS to serve students equally, it has to serve students who are not solely judged on how well they do in traditional face-to-face classes. Schools should work closely with LUDA-VHS personnel, site-coordinators, counselors, parents, and students in order to educate all parties in regard to what it takes to be an online student. Counselors should be trained to ensure that students who are approved or disapproved meet some of the criteria. If the student and parents feel strongly about taking an online class, the student should be allowed to enroll and try the online class for a short period. The student subsequently could be allowed to continue, pending his/her performance during that probationary period. Furthermore, as suggested by others who studied VHS projects (Kozma et al., 2000), in order for the project to have a broader impact, open access to online courses should be made available to all students, including students of limited English proficiency, students with disabilities, home schoolers, and at-risk students.

Teacher Training

Teachers need to receive training on how to develop and teach online classes. Two-day workshops do not provide enough time to prepare teachers to teach online. The workshop length needs to be extended in order to provide teachers the opportunities for practicing the principles of online teaching and learning. However, for teachers to be able to participate in longer training sessions will require the support of their school districts. Such support can include release time, reduced workload, and financial incentives. Teacher training can consist of a face-to-face component, where teachers meet with trainers to cover issues of online teaching, become familiar with the class Web site and its various components, and gain some knowledge on online teaching strategies. Training should continue online. During this period of training, teachers should practice what they have learned, continue reading articles on online learning, prepare their class syllabi, participate in collaborative projects with other teachers, and moderate discussions.

Teacher Compensation and Support

Consumer Education online was a new project for all schools involved. Therefore, participating schools did not have clear policies on how to handle teacher time, pay, and compensation. These issues are very important, and the LUDA Education Foundation and participating school districts need to establish clear policies on how to compensate and support teachers who want to participate in LUDA-VHS. Unless policies and expectations are clear, teachers will not support the project.

The results of this evaluation and our experience with distance learning over the last 15 years make us believe developing and teaching DE classes is not easy and oftentimes it is more time consuming than teaching a face-to-face class. One of the issues that became clear during the pilot project is that teachers cannot work full time, and, at the same time, develop online classes. Teachers need to be on sabbatical leave or have a reduced workload to be able to focus on developing online classes. Furthermore, teachers should be provided with ongoing support to ensure they have everything they need to teach online classes. For example, a mentor program can be established in which an expert online teacher mentors a first-time online teacher and provides her with support and help while she teaches an online class for the first time.

Site Coordinators

Several of the issues associated with LUDA-VHS can be resolved when site coordinators are trained and assigned to each participating school. Several of the suggested tasks recommended for the site coordinator are tasks that teachers will be performing. A site coordinator could be a counselor who will receive training in online classes and would also be able to provide guidance to students in choosing the right class. Each school should have a site coordinator. One of the site coordinators could be the district coordinator who would serve as the link between his/her district and LUDA-VHS. Site coordinators need to receive training similar to the training that teachers would receive in online teaching and learning. Some of the specific duties of the site coordinator could be the following:

1. Market the class in his/her school and recruit students.
2. Handle all administrative issues that relate to LUDA-VHS, such as student enrollment, class credit, grades, and the like.
3. Serve as the liaison between his/her school and LUDA-VHS.
4. Provide help and guidance to students.

5. Monitor student performance and communicate regularly with teachers.
6. Report to the school principal and superintendent with regard to the progress of the project and possible issues and problems that might arise.

LUDA-VHS as a Valid Venue for Education

DE and VHS projects are innovations that will take time for the general public to accept as valid venues for teaching and learning. School administrators are often reluctant to participate in efforts that might have an impact on their schools, particularly when the nature of that impact is unknown. Leaders from school districts and teachers need to be brought into such projects and be actively involved. To accomplish this, the LUDA Education Foundation should organize a campaign to educate personnel from other districts and the general public about LUDA-VHS and the benefits from participating in the project. For the interest in LUDA-VHS to grow among LUDA districts, the content for additional classes should be developed by school districts, other than the three that developed the content for Consumer Education. The sense of ownership should be spread out to as many districts as possible. When school districts develop the content, they will have a sense of ownership and be more committed to embracing the project.

Quality Assurance and Evaluation

As more classes are developed, more LUDA schools will join LUDA-VHS and the project will grow and expand to include large numbers of students. One major concern that emerges is quality assurance. In order to maintain high quality course development and instruction to LUDA high school students, the LUDA Education Foundation should establish a mechanism of regular review of its courses, content alignment with Illinois Learning Standards, and professional development opportunities for teachers. The results of every review should be shared with the districts to help them improve their contribution to the project.

CONCLUSION

LUDA-VHS was successful because a synergy of people, resources, and processes worked together in a team spirit, sharing the same vision. Alignment with school districts' technology plans, commitment and ownership to the project, high quality material, frequent teacher-student interaction, and good teamwork were the major reasons for project success. As the project expands to include more schools, teachers, and students, several issues need to be addressed for continued success. Such issues include training and compensating teachers, selecting and supporting students, developing instructional strategies for online learning, educating the public on the benefits of DE, providing equal access, and building quality assurance mechanisms.

REFERENCES

Berge, Z. L., & Collins, M. P. (Eds.). (1995). *Computer mediated communication and the online classroom.* Cresskill, NJ: Hampton Press.

Johnson, D. W. (1981). Student-student interaction: The neglected variable in education. *Educational Researcher, 10*(1), 5-10.

Kozma, R., Zucker, A., Espinoza, C., McGhee, R., Yarnall, L., Zalles, D., & Lewis, A. (2000). *The online course evaluation of the third year implementation 1999-2000.* Menlo Park, CA: SRI International.

Mason, R. (1994). *Using communications media in open and flexible learning.* London: Kogan Page.

National Center for Educational Statistics. (2001). *Internet Access in U.S. public schools and classrooms: 1994-2000.* Washington, DC: U.S. Department of Education.

Owston, R. D. (1997). The World-Wide-Web: A technology to enhance teaching and learning? *Educational Researcher, 26*(2), 27-32.

Vrasidas, C. (2000). Constructivism versus objectivism: Implications for interaction, course design, and evaluation in distance education. *International Journal of Educational Telecommunications, 6*(4), 339-362.

Vrasidas, C., & McIsaac, S. M. (1999). Factors influencing interaction in an online course. *The American Journal of Distance Education, 13*(3), 22-36.

Vrasidas, C., & McIsaac, M. (2000). Principles of pedagogy and evaluation of Web-based learning. *Educational Media International, 37*(2), 105-111.

Vrasidas, C., & Glass, G. V. (Eds.). (2002). *Distance education and distributed learning.* Greenwich, CT: Information Age Publishing.

J. Wanless Southwick

Distance Education in the Rural K-12 Environment

SUMMARY. A small rural school in Idaho tried various forms of distance education to broaden the range of subjects offered to students. It gave up on satellite-based coursework because of high cost and synchronization problems. Correspondence courses solved the synchronization problem, but still required expensive adult supervision to keep students on task. IP-based videoconferencing appeared to promise lower costs and better synchronization, but in practice it proved to be difficult to implement and exhausting for course teachers. The school began to view videoconferencing in terms of its enrichment and collaboration values. The Internet, together with other distance education technologies, may one day erase the educational disadvantages of rural isolation. They also promise to make lifelong learning the expected norm. *[Article copies available for a fee from The Haworth Document Delivery Service: 1-800-HAWORTH. E-mail address: <docdelivery@haworthpress.com> Website: <http://www.HaworthPress. com> © 2003 by The Haworth Press, Inc. All rights reserved.]*

KEYWORDS. Rural, school, satellite, cost, synchronization, supervision, videoconferencing, collaboration, enrichment, Internet

J. WANLESS SOUTHWICK is Educational Technology Director, Dietrich School District #314, Dietrich, ID 83324 (E-mail: jwanless@direcway.com).

[Haworth co-indexing entry note]: "Distance Education in the Rural K-12 Environment." Southwick. J. Wanless. Co-published simultaneously in *Computers in the Schools* (The Haworth Press, Inc.) Vol. 20, No. 3, 2003, pp. 27-32; and: *Distance Education: What Works Well* (ed: Michael Corry. and Chih-Hsiung Tu) The Haworth Press, Inc., 2003, pp. 27-32. Single or multiple copies of this article are available for a fee from The Haworth Document Delivery Service [1-800-HAWORTH, 9:00 a.m. - 5:00 p.m. (EST). E-mail address: docdelivery@haworthpress.com].

10.1300/J025v20n03_04

Our rural school district in Dietrich, Idaho, is isolated in a lava rock and sage-brush desert in southern Idaho. It has less than 200 total students, counting kindergarten through the 12th grade. Our school has always been the center of this sparsely populated agricultural community and is dear to the hearts of its patrons. When the threat of mandatory consolidation stirred in the state legislature in 1989, panic gripped the tiny town. Consolidation proponents harangued about funding equity and complained that small schools got more money per student but could only offer "a narrow range of subjects to children." Rural voices throughout the state rang out to extol the virtues of the personal nature of education in small schools. In the end, the controversy died out, with rural schools surviving, but stung by the criticism of their "narrow range of subjects" taught.

STAR SCHOOLS MODEL

When an opportunity to participate in distance education via satellite arrived in the early 1990s, our school jumped at the chance to use this new education technology to broaden the range of subjects that could be taught. We saw this technology as a way to overcome the disadvantages of isolation, but still keep the advantages of smallness. A separate building was converted into a "distance learning center." A satellite dish, receiver, large television set, and special speakerphone were set up for the classes. We were pleased that we could offer a Russian language course to a small group of high school students. We also liked the enrichment programs that came over the satellite dish. We were impressed with the quality of the teacher in-service sessions that came with the STAR Schools membership arrangement.

It was not long, however, before our enthusiasm for this style of distance education began to wane, largely due to the following:

1. *Cost.* Not only was there a membership fee to be part of the organization (e.g., STEP Star Schools), but there were also tuition payments for each student who took a class. Everything offered by satellite seemed to develop a price tag.
2. *Adult Supervision.* It was necessary to pay a teacher or an aide to be with students in the distance learning classroom. High school students didn't seem to be able to stay on task without adult oversight. The adult represented another cost.
3. *Schedule.* Satellite-based distance education works best when the remotely taught course occurs during a regular class period in the school day. Rarely could we synchronize schedules; therefore, disruption of the student routine or a wholesale shift of class scheduling had to be confronted. Even the commencement of the school year, beginning and ending dates of semesters, and vacation schedules complicated synchronization efforts.

CORRESPONDENCE COURSES

Sometimes we had students take Internet-based distance education classes on an individual basis. These classes were essentially electronic versions of correspondence courses. They helped us offer a way for certain students to meet graduation requirements. They also offered the promise of expanded course offerings for unique student needs. Since these classes were essentially asynchronous by design, we didn't have the scheduling problem, but cost and supervision problems remained. Again, there was significant evidence that high school students have a hard time staying on task without adult supervision.

IP-BASED VIDEOCONFERENCE SYSTEMS

Schools in our region of Idaho are building IP (H.323) based videoconferencing capacity for distance education. While these facilities seem to function well for teacher in-service sessions and other adult collaboration, their use for teaching remote high school students has been problematic:

1. Adult supervision of the remote classroom not only requires the prodding of students into attentiveness, but also the remote supervising adult needs to have a level of competence in both the content area being taught and in the workings of the videoconferencing technology.
2. Unreliable quality of the videoconference connection is a vexing inhibition to the success of distance education. A common problem is a lack of adequate bandwidth for "quality of service." Point-to-point videoconferencing seems to get by well with a T-1 line, but as more remote classrooms are connected to a videoconference, T-1 fails to supply enough bandwidth. The inability of teachers or classroom aides to troubleshoot hardware glitches exacerbates the problem.
3. Distance education requires more work on the part of the originating teacher. The extra work is not just the additional preparation to make a lesson plan work at a distance, but there is the challenge of operating the classroom hardware so that both local and remote students are fully engaged in the learning process. Teachers report that distance education is an exhausting experience.
4. The assumption that distance education is a handy way to offer a greater variety of coursework to more students at less cost is open to serious question.

So what good is videoconferencing for distance education in the K-12 environment? It can probably succeed if the extra work and associated expenses are recognized and compensated for. Suggestions include:

1. Having someone who can troubleshoot videoconferencing glitches available for both the originating and remote classrooms.
2. Placing an adult in the remote classroom who has some competence in the content area.
3. Compensating the originating teacher for extra preparation time.

ALTERNATIVE JUSTIFICATION

There are educational reasons for considering videoconferencing in the K-12 environment, other than creating traditional distance education classrooms. Videoconferencing becomes a powerful enrichment tool when used for "content area collaboration." A classic example was a demonstration that water boils differently at different altitudes. It was conducted by an elementary school class near sea level in Oregon, in partnership with a similar elementary class in the Rocky Mountains of Montana (NREL, 1999, 2000). Using standard scientific apparatus (an equal amount of water in a beaker with a thermometer, heated by a Sterno fuel source), students in each location were able to use videoconferencing links to watch simultaneous water boiling progress. The geographically separated students recorded water temperature rise each minute until the water started to boil. Then they needed to explain why the water boiled at different temperatures at their different elevations. This was not abstract science. Both schools could see the difference happening in real time. The demonstration's success was related to the content-area competency of the collaborating teachers and the skillful way they engaged their respective students in a science discovery project.

BROADBAND VIDEOCONFERENCE CONSORTIUM

The three small school districts in our rural county formed the Lincoln County Consortium of Schools to construct a broadband videoconferencing network. The only viable broadband option available to us was wireless. After many months of design work, we arranged to have consortium antennas placed on an existing communications tower, which is perched on top of a dormant volcano that sits near the middle of the county. Dish antennas on each school were aimed at the volcano tower to give 10 Mbps of bandwidth between schools for videoconferencing. An additional wireless link will hop 18 miles with 45 Mbps of bandwidth into the more populated part of southern Idaho to connect with larger schools and the Internet.

We discovered that H.323 videoconferencing that uses voice, video, *and* data is complicated to design. It involves not only videoconferencing hardware, but also networking issues such as maintaining firewall integrity and the use of multimedia conference managers (MCM), gatekeepers, proxy servers, network address translation (NAT), quality of service (QoS) control, and a multipoint control unit (MCU). No single vendor seemed to have all the answers for design and installation issues.

The consortium's approach to distance education includes the following goals:

1. Integrate new videoconferencing equipment into the curriculum of the three school districts.
2. Carefully align class schedules of consortium schools to permit resource sharing.
3. Use videoconferencing for in-service training of teachers, including how to integrate videoconferencing technologies into the curriculum.
4. Have each consortium district offer to teach at least one course to students in the other consortium schools via videoconferencing.
5. Encourage teachers of compatible curricula to use videoconferencing to collaborate with one another across district boundaries and to engage their respective students in meaningful "content-area collaboration" with videoconferencing. (For example, science teachers in each school might assign their respective students to research the same local environmental problem and propose possible solutions. The teachers could arrange for their students to collaborate via videoconference, exchange proposed solutions, and dialog about which proposal would be the best solution.)
6. Assess student achievement by gathering data to document improvements in student learning that result from educational videoconferencing. (In the above example, collaborating teachers could give the same test instrument to their respective students, before and after videoconference collaboration, to observe the improvement in learning.)
7. Help teachers find worldwide videoconferencing partners to enrich their content-area instruction and to help their students understand why they need to learn.
8. Cooperate with other regional schools to share instructional resources and to expand the coursework available to (and from) consortium schools.
9. Explore the options for these isolated teachers to take college-level classes by local videoconference to avoid the expense and hazards of long-distance travel.

CONCLUSION

If getting an education simply meant getting information, the Internet could be defined as distance education. But distance education, like any education, is more than simply encountering information. Effective distance education must be able to guide the learner, discern whether learning is taking place, and remove barriers to the learner's comprehension. These things are difficult to do without a live teacher. In the K-12 environment, students need the physical presence of an adult to make distance education work well.

The weaknesses of various distance education strategies include substantial costs for equipment and personnel, the challenge of synchronizing provider and learner schedules, the extra work required of the originating teacher, and the reliability of the delivery system (technology glitches).

The strengths of various distance education strategies include the promise to broaden the range of subjects that can be offered, access to education from almost anywhere at almost anytime, individualization of instructional strategies, and increased learner control over the educational outcome.

Distance education provides possible alternatives to the current factory model for K-12 education, with its incarceration factor and the tyranny of its class-period bell. Although the current model usually fits the working parent's need for child daycare, if technology creates more flexible work patterns for parents, distance education may provide more flexible educational alternatives for their children.

Videoconferencing technologies are maturing beyond simple "closed-circuit TV" links. Conferees are not only able to see and hear each other, but they can share ideas and data on an interactive computer screen at each conference location (e.g., the iPower software from PictureTel (now Polycom) with its "people + content" design). The application of these new technologies to distance education has profound implications. Teachers can entice students to learn in new and innovative ways. Teachers can use videoconferencing to expand the walls of their classroom to great distances. The peer audiences, with whom students interact, can cross many boundaries via videoconferencing. Videoconferencing can help skillful teachers manipulate the context for learning, thereby giving their students greater depths of understanding. Content-area collaboration, which is sponsored by peer teachers for their students in widely separated classes, may ultimately become one of the most important aspects of K-12 distance education.

If these distance education technologies continue to improve and decrease in cost, as they have in recent years, the successors to today's Internet and videoconferencing will make lifelong learning the expected norm. They may dim the distinction between student and employee. They may obscure our notions of graduation with academic degrees by increased focus on competency certifications. They may enrich our lives with expanded opportunities to pursue profitable alternatives or flights of fancy. They may largely erase the disadvantages of rural isolation.

REFERENCE

Northwest Regional Educational Laboratory. (1999/2000). Lights, camera, sterno! *NETC Circuit,* pp. 4-5. Portland, OR: Author.

Timothy R. Jenney
Eva K. Roupas

Quality Connection:
Going the Distance

SUMMARY. In 1999, Virginia Beach City Public Schools launched a completely new distance learning (DL) initiative, Quality Connection. Since that time, through perseverance and creative thinking, the program has become a model of technology as well as a highly successful method of delivering services to a wide variety of stakeholders. Not only do students reap benefits from Quality Connection, but also school and office staff and administrators use DL in numerous capacities. Indeed, Quality Connection is slated for replication by other school divisions in Virginia. Although the program was developed originally to offer expanded curricula to students and training opportunities for staff, DL has had the ancillary effect of reprising the division's long-term goals and revolutionizing short-term strategies. It is through the foresight and business acumen of division leadership that VBCPS maintains its motto, "Ahead of the Curve." *[Article copies available for a fee from The Haworth Document Delivery Service: 1-800-HAWORTH. E-mail address: <docdelivery@ haworthpress.com> Website: <http://www.HaworthPress.com> © 2003 by The Haworth Press, Inc. All rights reserved.]*

TIMOTHY R. JENNEY is Superintendent, Virginia Beach Public Schools, Virginia Beach, VA 23456-0038 (E-mail: tjenney@vbcps.k12.va.us).
EVA K. ROUPAS is Distance Learning Coordinator, Virginia Beach Public Schools, Virginia Beach, VA 23456-0038 (E-mail: ekroupas@vbcps.k12.va.us).

[Haworth co-indexing entry note]: "Quality Connection: Going the Distance." Jenney, Timothy R., and Eva K. Roupas. Co-published simultaneously in *Computers in the Schools* (The Haworth Press, Inc.) Vol. 20, No. 3, 2003, pp. 33-40; and: *Distance Education: What Works Well* (ed: Michael Corry, and Chih-Hsiung Tu) The Haworth Press, Inc., 2003, pp. 33-40. Single or multiple copies of this article are available for a fee from The Haworth Document Delivery Service [1-800-HAWORTH, 9:00 a.m. - 5:00 p.m. (EST). E-mail address: docdelivery@haworthpress.com].

http://www.haworthpress.com/store/product.asp?sku=J025
© 2003 by The Haworth Press, Inc. All rights reserved.
10.1300/J025v20n03_05

33

KEYWORDS. Distance learning, value-added, return on investment, cost avoidance, capital investment, master teachers, competitive parity, systemic change, "Ahead of the Curve"

What do you call a project that incubates for nearly 20 years, is free of cost in its development, and has the potential to solve basic student equity concerns regarding equal access to high level academic course work? We in Virginia Beach Schools call it "Quality Connection: Going the Distance." And our innovative distance learning project does–in 11 high schools and 5 middle schools– "go the distance."

Currently, 595 students spread across the division share teachers in 36 content-rich classes, that would otherwise not be available to students in their home schools, either because of teacher shortage or low student enrollment. Distance Learning (DL) prevents the cancellation of these courses needed by students and provides not only a return on financial investment but also value-added opportunity.

In the spring of 1998, Virginia Beach City Public Schools was approached by two enthusiastic vendors, Cox Communications and Dynamic Systems Integration (DSI). Cox was a cable company eager to create a potential market and at the same time provide a philanthropic service, while DSI, a systems contractor, was willing to provide the equipment, maintenance, and service to their community school system, Virginia Beach City Public Schools. Cox/DSI proposed working with our division for one year to design a three-point beta test site at no cost to the division for either equipment or cable lines. Our job as a school system was to make the concept work by developing one class to be offered via DL by the second semester of 1999.

Cox originally selected three schools in which to install equipment, all based upon the company's geographic plan to install fiber optic technology in the schools' corresponding neighborhoods. While this suited Cox's long-range design, it did not suit the division's, as the schools they chose were the three largest, each course-rich. In order for the initiative to be innovative and successful, we realized we had to include a high school where demographics demanded equity as well as parity with the other schools selected. Ultimately, Cox agreed with our philosophy and, in an ironic compromise, changed their cablevision installation schedule, causing an entire section of the community to receive the service a full year ahead of Cox's original design–and all as a result of the school division's Distance Learning initiative.

In preparation for the creation of our first class, we knew we had several critical components to consider: The first of these was deciding what class would be taught and which teacher would teach it. Once these issues were decided we had to find someone to coordinate all the details and design the all-important structured training protocol. We were well aware that Cox/DSI was investing heavily in our DL prototype and would be on board for at least one year. This fact relieved us somewhat from being overly tied to recruiting a technology expert. We knew also that anyone teaching to a camera in a virtual classroom must possess a very different set of skills than those required of a teacher in a traditional setting.

Consequently, we chose as our coordinator a teacher who was first and foremost a thespian. But not just any thespian. Our first choice was the 1998 teacher of the year for our district as well as a career drama teacher. Not only did she have the crucial ability to relate to our teachers and, therefore, market the program from a non-techie perspective, but she was also able to teach the teachers. She could teach them that most valuable lesson of being likeable and effective while teaching "long distance" through the camera lens and of being conversant while "wired." In short, she taught our teachers how to be master teachers in a virtual classroom.

Certainly, the medium of television in education is hardly new. Colleges and universities used television instruction in the '60s and '70s, albeit with a one-way delivery system. Even 20 years ago in northern Michigan, we conducted a feasibility study for using an ITFS (Instructional Television Fixed Service) microwave structure to deliver a DL product. The idea was good, but the timing was not. We found the technology too expensive to demonstrate a return on our investment. In addition, there wasn't the sense of urgency we now have to provide not only competitive course work but also a spectrum of choice. Over the years, one finds that vision is an interesting concept, especially when it concerns technology. Perhaps the metaphor of being on the "bleeding" edge of innovation is most apropos. A vision can easily turn into a nightmare. In Virginia Beach, however, we found that time does have a way of mitigating inherent risk as we made our vision a reality.

Technology in the classroom thus became our mantra, and creating the pilot project became a true collaboration with Cox Communication and Dynamic Systems Integration. Our DL coordinator, while training our teachers, also managed the project, keeping it on track and on time.

After deciding which of our three high schools to wire and what the first class should be (Discrete Mathematics–an advanced math class as it turned out), work ensued on technology installation at all sites. Rooms were similarly equipped and were designed as either origination or receiving sites. Equipment was permanently fixed in each school's dedicated DL room and consisted of several basic items. Among them were a primary camera that focused on the teacher, a touch pad to be operated by the teacher that allowed her to manipulate the equipment, and a document camera, also operated by the teacher, which focused on notes, books, papers, and the like. At the same time, the teacher was able to operate cameras at the remote sites, selecting the video sources viewed by the student. To enable the teacher to preview each image before it was broadcast, a special monitor was installed. In addition, each classroom was fitted with four television monitors, two at the front of the room and two further back.

The teacher was thus equipped to choose all images to be viewed on the monitors, whether it was the computer screen, a document via the document image camera, an instructional video, or even a shot from another camera.

At the corresponding receiving sites, students who had questions were able to press a button on the microphone installed at each desk/table. The remote site camera had the capability of zooming in on the student as the microphone amplified the question. The teacher and students at all sites could hear what was being asked and the teacher's response. A student who wanted to show the teacher his or her work could use the document camera installed at the receiving site.

The benefits incurred by such technology were immediately obvious. Classes taught at only one school could be broadcast to distant sites across the city. A teacher with special knowledge or skills could instruct students at our three sites across the city without additional travel time or expense. In addition, students no longer had to transfer to another school in order to take a class offered at that school only.

Comparative financial data are difficult to produce and incorporate certain assumptions about capital investments, class sizes, and, of course, the altruistic value which is added through course availability. On average, for equal enrollments of regular classes versus DL classes, it will be approximately one-third higher in cost per pupil in any given DL class. Taking into consideration the cost of a teacher assistant at each remote site, the expense will necessarily be more. For example, the regular cost per pupil for a Japanese class of 21 students is $464. The DL cost per pupil for the same 21 students at two sites will be $639.

What, then, are the advantages that make Distance Learning classes worth offering. Simply put, we believe that the real savings are associated with cost avoidance. Note that the example we gave addressed Japanese being offered at two separate sites. In the real world of secondary school scheduling, principals make decisions all the time to allow low enrollment classes to survive the cut line, sometimes at the expense of larger core courses. Offering a class of between 6-10 students is very inefficient, assuming that a teacher can even be found. Sometimes we make teachers travel between schools at an expense to the district and most of the time the teacher is given an extra period to make the trek. Losing a bell of instruction is a 20% loss in productivity.

The capital investment in the DL lab should be no different from the development of a science lab, a music lab, or even a language lab. It is a good exercise to create a comparative expense of Distance Learning along with the anomalies of regular class exceptions, to the extent possible. After all, someone is going to ask and it behooves you to get out in front of the nay sayers. Decisions can then be made as to cost efficiencies and the philosophical view of parity through a value-added approach. Our students, the main stakeholders, had the most to gain through DL opportunities, and the benefits to them were innumerable. For example, their choices of classes expanded greatly. Courses that were either inaccessible because they were offered at only one or two high schools, or not offered at all because of low enrollment, were now available. Students had the opportunity to enroll in more esoteric Advance Placement or upper level language classes they needed to improve their chances of admission into the more selective colleges and universities. In addition, problems of equity and fairness were equalized. Then and only then can a true picture emerge for financial decisions to be made.

This scenario was rapidly born out at two of our high schools. Students had wanted to enroll in AP physics and statistics, neither of which was offered at their home schools. However, by employing DL, two other high schools originated these courses, thus allowing the students who needed and wanted them to enroll. The increased opportunity also helped the division market itself to students who otherwise might have enrolled in private schools, simply because they needed higher level courses not available in our local public schools.

It is a truism that good teachers will rally to fill student academic needs. Certainly, we found this to be true in Virginia Beach. However, while student need was a main factor in course and teacher selection, there were several other crucial determiners as well. Some might consider them to be self-serving, but the end result was the establishment of a firm foundation for distance learning across the division. We were able to "sell" distance learning to some principals and teachers because of differing agendas. Among these agendas were the following: avoiding involuntary transfers due to low enrollments; generating interest in fledgling programs that needed a jumpstart; and saving dangerously low enrollment elective courses that were close to being dropped from the master schedule.

We made a conscious decision to be inclusive of all who were interested in providing DL instruction, and that has proven to be a wise choice. We have been pleased with the vast majority of the experiences provided for both our teachers and students. We have found that often DL experiences tended to provide motivation for those students who were previously unmotivated or unprepared.

Not unlike the students, our teachers came to the DL program at various stages of their careers. They, too, had various motivating factors. Career stimulation, interest in preserving their course work, and, in some cases, genuine curiosity were but a few of those factors. However, whatever the reason, we found that, once these teachers had completed their instruction of a videoconferenced class, they were "hooked." A sampling of the comments made by our DL teachers included such endorsements as: "The technology has made me a better, organized, thorough teacher" and "I love the innovativeness and inventiveness of the equipment," as well as "A document camera should be included in every teacher's classroom." Several other teachers wrote, "My other (non-DL) classes are reaping the benefits of my DL instruction," and "This gives me another opportunity to teach differently. My teaching style has shifted and I'm thinking of activities/presentations that I hadn't thought of."

As our program has grown, we are now able to answer more directly to the needs of the schools and recruit specific teachers that have been recommended by our instructional coordinators. As a result, we are continuing to provide students with broader exposure to our "master teachers" and all they have to offer.

DL requires involvement at all levels. Central office curriculum staff, building level principals, and classroom teachers had mixed feelings about the introduction of DL in their routine schedules. It was both a boon and a curse to some of them. It is a given that each school develops its own culture and its own traditions. Change disturbs that balance. Add to that mix the reality that staff allocations are typically designed with the building teachers in mind. It is easy to understand how DL interrupted that balance and caused initial discomfort. Using technology as a teaching tool is improving with most teachers. However, use of technology is more than a philosophical transmission of instruction. Teachers must now operate the equipment and learn the control board, which requires an incredible stretch regarding their own capabilities. Finally, it must be realized that a DL classroom is a very public place. No one "owns" the classroom, or program. Anyone who happens to walk into the DL room can see and hear the operational practices. This means that no school is able to maintain primacy or privacy.

Convincing high school principals to make their master schedules flexible, offer the services of their respective staffs to other schools, and dedicate a whole classroom to DL was a bit like asking Chrysler to offer their latest auto designs to Ford, just because it was "good for the economy." As one can imagine, we used all the typical management tools to convince principals it was "good for the school division." Among our strategies were begging, pleading, bullying, and threatening–figuratively speaking. In essence, we did require principals to adhere to minimum and maximum class sizes, which, in turn, created need. In addition, we thanked and praised those who positively effected change and worked with and around those who became impediments.

But success breeds success. After two and a half years, most of our principals are not only relatively comfortable with the concept, but they also have taken pride and ownership in the project. To our staff members' and administrators' credit, they understand the student-centeredness of DL, the vast opportunities DL provides, and the cost effectiveness of the technology. We are now targeting competitive parity with regular education (traditional) classes. Although the value added concept will never go away, people are looking for a common standard of comparison on a per pupil cost. The program has ultimately been accepted, one school at a time. DL has earned the acceptance it deserves and further expansion has received the green light.

Also critical to the success of the program have been two components: first, strong, unwavering visible support from the school board and upper level administration; and, second, having a DL coordinator who facilitated and supported the program as the staff and students adjusted to this new venue for instruction. With the successful launching of our first DL class and the resulting acceptance by students, teachers, administrators, and parents, expansion of the program was assured.

The first year, 20 students received DL instruction. By the second year we increased enrollment by 220%. The next increase was 278%, and in school year 2000-2001, the jump was 115%. In the fall of 2001, we had a 22% increase for a total of 369 students. Plans call for a further increase for second semester.

Student enrollment was another variable that was a challenge to us for a variety of reasons. The more sites a teacher instructed, the more potentially cost effective the program was. However, it was important to canvas all the sites and restrict the numbers of students and sites taught in order not to lose the value added piece of our DL instruction. Through trial and error, as well as through learning from a school district with an ITV (interactive television) program in place for several years in Wisconsin, we found the target caps needed to be 25 students per class at no more than four sites. It must be noted, however, that we evaluate each course on a case-by-case basis and our program is too young for these numbers to be absolute.

However, DL technology remains a moving target. We have in three years installed the technology in all 11 high schools and five middle schools, with plans to wire the final 10 middle schools by 2004. Additional expansion plans call for using DL for further staff development, for student tutoring, SAT and Standards of Learning (state-mandated yearly tests) prep classes, and teacher training. We also intend to take advantage of "neighboring" videoconferencing within the region, state, country, and even the world. Previously we have set up a dialogue between high school seniors and Stanford University admissions officers and hosted a sister-city connection with North Down, Bangor, Ireland. The recruiting arm of our Human Resources Department has also conducted interviews with prospective teachers at colleges and universities in other states. Currently, we are continuing to research and plan national and international symposiums. In addition to the sister city connections with North Down, Bangor, Ireland, in February 2001, one of our high schools had our forty top high-achieving high school juniors have a virtual meeting with the Vice Provost of Undergraduate Studies from Stanford University to discuss college applications. We are also participating with our local public television station, WHRO, and neighboring cities in order to eventually collaborate in creating a Virtual Regional High School.

We found, however, that creating our DL reality was the best of times and worst of times. Once we navigated the first year, we realized the initiative would require a sizeable investment on the part of the school division. To comply with school board regulations, this meant the project had to go out to bid, which presented a rather ticklish public relations problem with the company that had so far been our benefactor, Cox Communication. After all, they had invested nearly $250,000 in time and equipment, and we had to tell them to get in line with everyone else. Perhaps some things are just meant to be: Cox/DSI was awarded the competitive bid for DL technology in Virginia Beach Schools. As a result, we have been able to expand our services seamlessly to additional schools.

What is the future for Virginia Beach City Public Schools with distance learning? We suspect it will continue to be an evolutionary process. Using the Internet–and Intranet–is the next obvious step. Asynchronous/virtual classes or perhaps even schools are no longer a distant reality. The beauty of this current initiative, however, is not the technology itself, but the attitude and impulse to embrace the possibility that there may be a better way to conduct business. There always has been a better way, but we are of a profession that does not accept systemic change easily. We believe we have found a way to bring people and technology together to create not only a better product but a better student. Put another way, "quality connection" has made it possible for us to "go the distance."

Marina Stock McIsaac
Elizabeth Harris Craft

Faculty Development: Using Distance Education Effectively in the Classroom

SUMMARY. This article outlines best practices for teachers who are faced with the often-daunting task of teaching online using the World Wide Web. In many cases, these instructors are asked to design, develop and implement a Web-based or Web-enhanced course in a short period of time. Often administrators and faculty alike are unaware of the preparation time needed to effectively design and deliver a quality distance course. This article offers guidelines and suggests useful resources in the areas of: providing faculty orientation, designing the online syllabus, building a social community of learners, and moderating online discussions to improve interactivity. These key strategies are crucial to successfully directing students through the provision of quality online learning experiences. Web links are provided to guide the reader through the process. *[Article copies available for a fee from The Haworth Document Delivery Service: 1-800-HAWORTH. E-mail address: <docdelivery@haworthpress. com> Website: <http://www.HaworthPress.com> © 2003 by The Haworth Press, Inc. All rights reserved.]*

MARINA STOCK McISAAC is Professor Emeritus, Educational Technology, Arizona State University, Tempe, AZ 85287-0611 (E-mail: mmcisaac@asu.edu).
ELIZABETH HARRIS CRAFT is Director, Distance Learning Technology, Arizona State University, Tempe, AZ 85287-0611 (E-mail: elizabeth.craft@asu.edu).

[Haworth co-indexing entry note]: "Faculty Development: Using Distance Education Effectively in the Classroom." McIsaac, Marina Stock, and Elizabeth Harris Craft. Co-published simultaneously in *Computers in the Schools* (The Haworth Press, Inc.) Vol. 20, No. 3, 2003, pp. 41-49; and: *Distance Education: What Works Well* (ed: Michael Corry, and Chih-Hsiung Tu) The Haworth Press, Inc., 2003, pp. 41-49. Single or multiple copies of this article are available for a fee from The Haworth Document Delivery Service [1-800-HAWORTH, 9:00 a.m. - 5:00 p.m. (EST). E-mail address: docdelivery@haworthpress.com].

10.1300/J025v20n03_06

KEYWORDS. Distance education, online learning, teacher training, Web-based learning, Internet

Educators are witnessing the rapid expansion of distance education delivery systems. Technologies such as video, CD, DVD, desktop conferencing and the Internet are used to distribute course materials that are marketed to educators. Schools that do not have their own resources to teach advanced courses in foreign language, math, or science can make use of these services to fill gaps in their curriculum. Teachers are often expected to integrate technologies using Web-enhanced or Web-based materials into their classes when they have had little experience doing so. At the same time, students may elect to take entire courses at a distance, or supplement their face-to-face courses with distance components, allowing them to work anytime/anyplace. In many cases the materials may be stand-alone courses or supplemental classroom materials that are print-based, media-based, or electronic. In all of these situations, teachers will need to have experience in teaching with technology. In a recent survey of 71 Nobel Laureates from the United States, United Kingdom, France, Germany, and Sweden, more than half believed that most students will likely be educated in virtual classrooms by the year 2020 [McMahon, 2002].

Recently, e-learning has entered the distance education marketplace. With the rapid development of computer networks, schools and universities have worked quickly to offer support to faculty in adopting new technologies and new ways of teaching. If technology-based curricular materials are to be useful, teachers must understand how to use them, feel at ease with them, and be motivated to incorporate them into their lessons. In a recent issue of *e-Learn* magazine, experts in distance education were polled for their predictions about electronic learning for 2002. Tony Bates, director of distance education at the University of British Columbia, echoed the sentiments of others when he said that most prestigious U.S. universities will adopt some form of broadband applications, and that corporate involvement in university e-learning will increase [Neal, 2002]. Faculty will be encouraged to use a variety of teaching methods, incorporating technology to allow students greater flexibility and access to classes. Most universities and schools will use technology to offer distance education options. These will all require a technology-literate faculty. Effective faculty development is at the heart of successful technology implementation.

At Arizona State University, the Distance Learning and Technology group has taken positive steps to provide faculty with assistance in designing, developing, and delivering both Web-based and Web-enhanced courses. A series of guidelines identifying best practices for delivering quality online courses is provided to faculty [Arizona State University, 2001]. These guidelines are directed toward providing information for instructors who are beginning to teach online, to help them plan and develop quality instruction. This article provides excerpts and selected guidelines from the longer document. Annotated online references to valuable links are located in the Appendix to this article.

Online links have proven useful to faculty as working resources in their search to design and deliver quality online courses. The links are dynamic and allow access to important concepts anytime/anyplace. They contain strategies unique to the online classroom. These documents contain guidelines, actual courses, strategies, and techniques to help prepare the new instructor for the important differences between online and traditional teaching. The following four categories have been found to be useful in helping faculty navigate the online learning environment: providing orientation for faculty designing the online syllabus, building a social community of learners, and moderating discussions to improve interactivity.

PROVIDING ORIENTATION FOR FACULTY

Teaching online is very different from teaching in a presenced, or face-to-face, environment. Plans must be made far in advance of the beginning of class. If complete and well-thought-out plans are in place, the course flows smoothly. The online classroom has different dynamics than the traditional class. The audience may be more mature, often consisting of adult re-entry learners. Before designing the course, instructors should identify the audience. Are the students first-time computer users? Have they had previous experience taking online classes?

Not only are students different, but teaching is different in an online environment. Students expect to participate in their learning experiences to a greater extent than in traditional situations. They become team members in the search for knowledge. The teacher in an asynchronous classroom goes beyond the blackboard. Lectures are not the primary means for constructing knowledge. In fact, the case is quite the opposite. The teacher in an asynchronous classroom should be a facilitator and is often a "guide on the side" rather than a "sage on the stage." A good teacher should provide guidance for online resources, encourage students to search widely, and build strategies for sharing resources. Active student-centered techniques and constructive learning experiences are integral to the online class.

Teaching and learning in a technology-based environment require support for both students and faculty in using technology as well as learner support for academic content. Where will students and faculty find answers late at night or early in the morning when most online work occurs? Faculty should identify those support services early in their planning.

DESIGNING THE ONLINE SYLLABUS

Since the online environment has few nonverbal cues to guide instructor and student, instructions must be built into the syllabus to ensure that both faculty and students know what lies ahead and exactly what is expected. Because misunderstandings can occur more easily at a distance, the syllabus must contain not only complete instructions, but also directions to students and faculty about where they can find technology support, and learning support. Since not all students participate online during normal business hours, provisions for support must be made for early mornings and late evenings.

The most important first step is to build a complete and well-designed syllabus. A good online syllabus is essential for a successful course. It is the roadmap that will be used by instructor and students. All of the interactions during the course will be based on information available in the syllabus, the information headquarters for all participants. If directions are changed during the semester, students who have worked ahead will be frustrated. The flexibility offered by a syllabus designed well in advance is one of the strengths of such a distance education course. Whether the course is open entry/open exit or synchronous week by week, many students want the flexibility of working ahead to accommodate their personal schedules. The syllabus that anticipates student needs will have readings, resources, discussion questions, online group identification, due dates for projects, test dates, and help strategies clearly mapped out. There are four components to successful online syllabi:

1. Dates that readings are due, and that topics will be discussed,
2. Readings with imbedded links and active resource lists,
3. Discussions with procedures detailed, and
4. Assignments and tests explained, procedures for help in place.

The syllabus must be available well ahead of class. It is useful in promoting the course and informing students about the course expectations and deadlines. Students who take online courses do not benefit from regular face-to-face reminders, so the syllabus becomes the document of agreement between instructor and student.

BUILDING A SOCIAL COMMUNITY OF LEARNERS

The social community supporting the individual online learner is one of the most important aspects of a successful online class. Students will be won or lost in the first few days of class. Those instructors who can create a warm, inviting social setting for students are more likely to know when someone is having technical, learning, or personal problems that impede successful course completion. Other students in the class form the basis for the community, and often are the catalysts for developing friendships that extend well beyond the completion of the course. Students who are having trouble will more easily turn to their peers for assistance. The enemy of the online class is student isolation. The friend is a strong sense of community. Each class develops its own unique community, coming together in collaborative work. The successful instructor encourages the development of an online intellectual and social community. This should be done early in the course by encouraging students to share information about themselves, their background, and their interests. Instructors should provide an informal atmosphere for this exchange. Many students are intimidated when they first write online. A good ice-breaker is posting biographies and photographs on the course site. Another effective strategy is to organize collaborative groups early in the course. These can be done around class topics and changed throughout the semester so students get to know everyone in the class. These collaborative assignments serve a number of purposes. The group work makes each person responsible for a portion of the final result. It also identifies strengths of each person. For example, some may be good writers, some may be technical gurus, still others have their unique perspectives that bring a richness to online discussions.

MODERATING DISCUSSIONS
TO IMPROVE INTERACTIVITY

Asynchronous discussions are the heart of the online course. If discussions are well planned and thoughtfully moderated, this is where the intellectual exchange of ideas occurs. Discussions should occur online after the reading for that topic has been done. Many teachers find that having students themselves post questions from the readings, and moderate the discussions, is a successful way to get greater participation from all members of the class. Students will engage more easily with peers, and they will take more responsibility for participation if all members take turns. It works best to model the intellectual level of discussion expected, making clear the number of contributions a student is expected to make in a specified period of time. Research has shown that discussions are more robust when they are moderated by students with occasional input from the instructor, than when moderated by the teacher alone (Vrasidas & McIsaac, 1999).

One goal of the online class is to foster interactivity. Interactivity can occur between student and instructor and between students themselves. Interactivity also takes place between students and course content as a part of the learning process. One goal of the effective online teacher is to promote interactive learning in as many areas as possible, using the strengths of the delivery system. In online situations, discussion folders, group folders, chat areas, and online office hours provide opportunities for these types of interaction.

CONCLUSION

The role of the teacher is changing. What was once regarded as distance education is now becoming part of mainstream education. The lecture mode of teaching was developed years ago to meet the needs of a different audience. New environments, such as the synchronous online class, are calling for new relationships between teacher and learner. The teacher as content expert will evolve as relationships change between teacher and student. Patterns of learning based on new settings and new relationships will emerge. Teachers will become designers of learning environments in their own disciplines, and students will shift into the role of information gatherers. This is already occurring as we see students now using the World Wide Web for research. They are finding information to create knowledge with the guidance of good teachers. Thus, the strategies and relationship between teachers and students will continue to evolve. Teachers who will be most influential will be those who can adapt to changing learning situations and who can use their expertise in the design of successful new learning environments.

REFERENCES

Arizona State University (2001). Best practices for delivering quality online courses, Distance Learning & Technology Group. Retrieved January 10, 2003, from http://asuonline.asu.edu/FacultySupport/ResourceCenter.cfm

McMahon, T. E. (2002). Internet will have important effect on global education: Nobel laureates, *Europemedia.net*. Retrieved February 5, 2002, from http://www.europemedia.net/shownews.asp?ArticleID=8175

Neal, L. E. (2002). Education and technology in perspective. *E-learn Magazine*. Published by the Association for Computing Machinery. Retrieved January 8, 2002, from http://www.elearnmag.org/

Vrasidas, C., & McIsaac, M. S. (1999). Factors influencing interaction in an online course. *The American Journal of Distance Education, 13*(3): 22-36.

APPENDIX
Selected, Annotated Online References by Topic

Orientation for Faculty

http://leahi.kcc.hawaii.edu/org/tcc_conf97/pres/pitt.html
Creating Powerful Online Courses Using Multiple Instructional Strategies.
Paper delivered in 1997 provides wide variety of strategies that can be used in
online classes. Research paper, good references.

http://coe.sdsu.edu/eet/
The Encyclopedia of Educational Technology (EET) is a collection of short
multimedia articles on a variety of topics (cognition and learning, analysis, design, development, implementation, evaluation) related to the fields of instructional design, education, and training. These background articles have useful
references to assist in the design and development of Web-based courses.

http://education2.edte.utwente.nl/teletophomepage.nsf/PapersNLViewForm?
readform
*Implementing Change Involving WWW-Based Course Support Across the
Faculty.* Written by B. A. Collis, Faculty of Educational Science and Technology, University of Twente. Research paper that outlines success factors in
creating institutional change through TeleTOP project. Identifies 9 success
factors for change to occur. Useful for planning change involving integration
of technology.

http://illinois.online.uillinois.edu/resources/
Illinois Online Network (ION) has a useful newsletter, and supports faculty
interested in online teaching and learning. The online resources section has
links to various aspects of online education. Includes online learning overview, conferences, organizations, tutorials, online Web design, instructional
design, and evaluation. An excellent resource.

http://illinois.online.uillinois.edu/IONresources/technology/myths.html
Seven Original Myths of Educational Technology, as formulated by Bill
Scroggins, past president, Academic Senate for California Community Colleges. The site has information about instructional design and online course
development techniques that are useful for the novice online teacher.

http://www-icdl.open.ac.uk/lit2k/
The International Centre for Distance Learning, affiliated with the British
Open University, was one of the first to collect documentation about open and

distance learning. This database contains information on over 30,000 distance courses and programs offered in Commonwealth countries, including Africa, Australia and Canada.

http://www.tafe.sa.edu.au/lsrsc/one/natproj/tal/
A description of teaching and learning styles that facilitate online learning.

http://www.fgcu.edu/onlinedesign/
Planning for course management during design and development may help reduce workload through better course planning. This is a resource for faculty who are designing online instructional materials.

http://www.knowledgeability.biz/weblearning/
This Web-based learning resources library offers links for the delivery and management of online learning. This is an excellent resource of links to topics of interest to those developing Web-based classes.

The Online Syllabus

http://valencia.cc.fl.us/
Valencia Community College provides online syllabus guidelines as part of their faculty orientation. The guidelines include a valuable checklist that is useful for traditional course syllabi that have been modified for online delivery.

http://ollie.dcccd.edu/Faculty/InfoForFaculty/DistrictResources/secure/olsyll2.htm
The Online Course Syllabus–Dallas Telecollege–complete guide to learning objectives and activities for online courses. Some useful suggestions for developing online course syllabi and links about online technical support and help.

http://www.aln.org/alnweb/magazine/issue2/knox.htm
The Pedagogy of Web Site Design by E. L. Skip Knox. A 1997 report of one teacher's design and pedagogy for a virtual course. A report from the trenches, a consideration of how static Web pages contribute to the creation of a successful online course.

https://courses.worldcampus.psu.edu/public/atb3/syllabustemplate/syllabus.html
Syllabus Writing 101, a template for setting up an online syllabus from Penn State World Campus, a leader in distance education. Each section contains specific guidelines, suggestions, and some examples to help people in the course planning process.

Social Community of Learners

http://www.elearningpost.com/elthemes/comm.asp
This article in e-learning provides information on building and sustaining online learning communities. It has links to best practices and other resources.

http://www.ion.illinois.edu/IONresources/conferencing/index.html
Strategies to promote communication online are given. Other topics are strategies for providing feedback, and grading participation in online courses.

http://www.aln.org/alnweb/journal/vol2_issue1/wegerif.htm
This paper describes the social importance of community for asynchronous learners. Factors affecting a student's sense of community are described.

Moderating Discussions

http://www.emoderators.com/moderators.shtml
Resources for Moderators and Facilitators of Online Discussion. This page is a set of resources for moderators and moderators-to-be of online discussions in both academic and non-academic settings. It includes links to the full text of articles and other resources related not only to the moderating but also the topics of "computer conferencing" and online teaching.

http://www.indiana.edu/~ecopts/ectips.html
Effectively Using Electronic Conferencing. Included here are Linda Harasim's suggestions and reference to the Global Network that are meant to stimulate readers' thinking about using electronic conferencing in their courses. It also provides additional resources that are good for getting ideas about effectively using electronic conferencing.

Chih-Hsiung Tu
Michael Corry

Building Active Online Interaction via a Collaborative Learning Community

SUMMARY. Online interaction creates a desirable learning situation. Transferring traditional instruction to an online environment usually does not generate effective interaction for learning. This paper discusses theories and practices for an interactive collaborative learning community in an online environment. Three theoretical constructs–interactivity, social context, and technologies–are discussed to provide a theoretical foundation. Effective online interactive strategies and activities, communications, online discussions, technology selections, peer evaluations, team moderations, team projects/presentations, and online learning specialists are recommended to maximize online learning interaction. *[Article copies available for a fee from The Haworth Document Delivery Service: 1-800-HAWORTH. E-mail address: <docdelivery@haworthpress.com> Website: <http://www.HaworthPress.com> © 2003 by The Haworth Press, Inc. All rights reserved.]*

KEYWORDS. Learning community, online collaboration, interaction, computer-mediated communication, active learning, distance education, e-learning, online moderation, teamwork, small group instructional design

CHIH-HSIUNG TU is Assistant Professor, Department of Educational Leadership, Educational Technology Leadership Program, The George Washington University, Washington, DC 20052 (E-mail: ctu@gwu.edu).
MICHAEL CORRY is Assistant Professor, Department of Educational Leadership, Educational Technology Leadership Program, The George Washington University, Washington, DC 20052 (E-mail: mcorry@gwu.edu).

[Haworth co-indexing entry note]: "Building Active Online Interaction via a Collaborative Learning Community." Tu, Chih-Hsiung, and Michael Corry. Co-published simultaneously in *Computers in the Schools* (The Haworth Press, Inc.) Vol. 20, No. 3, 2003, pp. 51-59; and: *Distance Education: What Works Well* (ed: Michael Corry, and Chih-Hsiung Tu) The Haworth Press, Inc., 2003, pp. 51-59. Single or multiple copies of this article are available for a fee from The Haworth Document Delivery Service [1-800-HAWORTH. 9:00 a.m. - 5:00 p.m. (EST). E-mail address: docdelivery@haworthpress.com].

10.1300/J025v20n03_07

Active online interaction remains a desirable learning situation. It has been said that "no interaction" equals "no learning" (Gunawardena, 1995). Online communication and interaction differ from traditional encounters because they are text-based and lack social context cues. Therefore, computer-mediated communication (CMC) requires different communication styles. Social context, online technology, and interactivity (Tu & Corry, 2002) are critical elements of online instruction. The purpose of this paper is to provide strategies to enhance online interaction via an active collaborative learning community design. These strategies and suggestions may be applied to increase the level of online interaction and, thereby, learning.

THEORETICAL BACKGROUND

The theoretical foundation for building a sustainable interactive collaborative online learning community via various technologies relies on three major constructs: interactivity, social context, and technologies (Tu & Corry, 2002). Interactivity incorporates concepts and designs that engage learners in active collaboration activities. Social context refers to the concepts of a learner-centered learning community. The third construct, technologies, supports and enhances knowledge development and knowledge management. These three constructs blend and overlap to the extent that one cannot implement one construct without including the other two. A key concept, a sense of "community," is also necessary to implementing online collaborative learning.

Interactivity

In collaborative learning small groups of students are encouraged to work together to maximize their own learning and the learning of each group member. Collaborative learning engages students in knowledge sharing, inspiring one another, depending upon one another, and applying active social interaction. Therefore, collaborative learning is an artistic rather than a mechanical process: "Collaborative learning (CL) is a personal philosophy, not just a classroom technique. In all situations where people come together in groups, it suggests a way of dealing with people, which respects and highlights individual group members' abilities and contributions. There is a sharing of authority and acceptance of responsibility among group members for the group's actions" (Panitz, 1996). Under the auspices of ideal collaborative learning, instructors shift their authority to the learners. Instructors also provide the foundation and learning structures to guide learners through various learning experiences involving active social interaction by applying modern technology. Gerdy (1998) states that "Good learning, like good work, is collaborative and social, not competitive and isolated; sharing one's ideas and responding to others' (ideas) improves thinking and deepens understanding."

Studies have shown that small-group instruction positively impacts student achievement, persistence, attitude, modeling, cognitive disequilibrium, cognitive development, self-esteem, social skills and the work of women and minorities (Johnson, Johnson & Holubec, 1990; Ocker & Yaverbaum, 1999; Slavin, 1991; Springer, Stanne & Donovan, 1997; Stahl & VanSickle, 1992; Stahl, 1994). However, when CMC is compared to face-to-face communication, no significant differences have been demonstrated in learning quality (Scifres, Gundersen & Behara, 1998) or on final exam grades (Benbunan-Fich & Hiltz, 1999).

Social Context

Social context emphasizes the characteristics of learners and the social learning environment (learning community). Collaboration is inherently social (Golub, 1988; Ocker & Yaverbaum, 1999). A social group values the members' obligations to one another. Team members support one another and their group because they feel it is the morally appropriate action (Jarvenpaa, Knoll, & Leidner, 1998). This sense of obligation to and support for one another are characteristic of online learners. Latham and Lock (1991) found that a group member skilled in self-management, goal setting, self-monitoring, and self-assessment is critical to the successful performance of the group. It also has been observed that successful groups are committed to the mission of the group, can be counted upon to perform their respective tasks, and enjoy working in a group (Snow, Snell & Davison, 1996). A successful online collaborative learning community is an organization where community members engage intellectually, mentally, socioculturally, and interactively in various structured and unstructured activities to achieve their common learning goals via electronic communication technologies.

Technologies

Technologies are important tools in human learning. Technology delivers content (information) and possesses the capability to stimulate opportunities for knowledge development. Many people prefer computer technology communication tools, like CMC, to face-to-face communication. Technologies such as e-mail, bulletin board, listserv, and real-time discussion are powerful tools for human communication. This is true in education communication; in fact, contents, bits, learning, and cognitive science are converging into "knowledge media" (Eisenstadt, 1995). Cooper (1998) identified technology as the most important issue in small-group learning and argued that technology-based instruction would have the most profound impact on student outcomes. Technologies that foster learner engagement with content, including techniques that encourage greater learner-learner and learner-teacher interaction, will comprise the classrooms of the future. Simply making technologies available for learners is not enough for nontraditional learners in the online collaborative learning process and the appropriate technical design of computing technologies is critical (Ocker & Yaverbaum, 1999).

PLAN, ORGANIZE, AND MANAGE

Developing an ideal online learning environment requires planning, organizing, and managing skills. To insure a good learning experience, an ideal interactive online learning environment requires a fully integrated design rather than a sparse collection of unrelated, disconnected, and fragmented learning activities scattered throughout the course. The importance of an online learning "community" is emphasized because it is the key to online collaborative learning. Fostering and building a community requires commitment, time, and long-term planning.

Simply copying the strategies outlined here will not result in an ideal learning experience; any successful online program must be fully integrated. Readers may adopt the entire group of activities discussed in this paper or they may select useful examples to incorporate into their own instructional design.

Communications

The foundation of an effective interactive online collaborative learning community is communication. Instructors should initiate the course with a definition of an online collaborative learning community and explain its purposes and expectations to motivate learners to sustain online learning collaboration throughout the course.

The instructor must communicate regularly, via e-mail or other computer-mediated communication forms, with every team and each individual throughout the course to provide support and to monitor progress. A mid-semester team report can be integrated to supply information that may be missed by simple observation. Instructors must attend discussions and team communications to provide psychological and substantive support. This process provides the instructor with information about the progress of the teams and permits early corrective intervention. Active participation may not be necessary; a simple demonstration of social presence by the instructor may be adequate.

Online Discussions

Synchronous and/or asynchronous online discussions are the core component in the online learning environment. Learners are required to participate as individuals in course discussions rather than as team members. A large class generates a large volume of messages that require reading and responses. This burden may be overwhelming to the students and provoke them to skip messages or withdraw from discussions. Much less difficulty is encountered if large groups are subdivided into smaller groups/teams for online discussions.

Selection of Technologies

It is more effective to make all of the multiple communication technologies available to online learners. Learners exhibit different communication styles in different places, at different times, and in different situations, making it advisable to permit them to select the communication technology with which they are most comfortable. Instructors should permit learners some laterality in determining what communication forms are used for class activities and team activities. The most frequently used technologies are bulletin board, real time chat, and e-mail. However, other technologies are also available, such as listserv, listserv digest, video-conferencing, and audio-conferencing.

Assignments

Online instruction engages learners in different assignment activities to assess if they are attaining the learning objectives. Very often, assignments are designed as individual activities that require learners to work alone with limited support from classmates. However, when students are allowed and encouraged to obtain support from peers, assignments become social exercises while maintaining the original objectives. This may enhance assignment performance and will permit the addition of peer evaluation activities.

Learners produce two drafts of an assignment in this design, first draft and final draft. The first draft is distributed to teammates, who review the assignment draft and return it with constructive comments. Peer feedback is also utilized in the preparation of the final draft, which is submitted for assessment. This collaboration involves students in three rich learning processes: preparing a first draft, providing constructive feedback, and preparing a final revision, utilizing the comments of peers.

Team Moderators

Engaging teams in moderating online discussions enriches learning responsibilities. Each team is responsible for online discussions of at least one lesson, which it selects. The team prepares discussion questions based on required readings, or assignments by the instructor, and moderates the discussion according to guidelines provided by the instructor. The discussion questions must be posted before the lesson begins, and the team initiates discussions that encourage classmates to participate, challenge the thinking of fellow learners, exchange information, and stimulate critical thinking. The team posts a summary of the discussion when the moderation responsibilities have been completed.

Team Projects

Assigning team projects is a common design in collaborative learning. Teams are required to post/upload their final products online for other teams to review. When the team project is completed, it is presented to the class using Microsoft PowerPoint or other authoring applications, and defended online, using bulletin board discussion or real-time chat.

Final Projects

Final projects can be designed like regular assignments; learners engage in draft preparation, peer review, feedback, and final draft preparation. The integration of an online presentation format into an individual final project requires learners to post/upload their final projects, to present them, and to defend them to their peers.

Team project presentation and individual final project presentation can be done either asynchronously or synchronously, depending upon the learning objectives, subjects, teaching styles, student learning styles, various learning situations, availability of various communication technologies, and time.

Online Learning Specialists

Instructors invite the participation of local, national, or international specialists in fields that are appropriate to the course content and learning objectives. These online learning specialists engage teams of learners as rich learning resources via e-mail or other communication technologies. These specialists are contacted by teams, as opposed to individuals, to prevent them from becoming overwhelmed by volumes of online messages. The instructor must provide etiquette guidelines in communicating with these specialists. After a team receives a response from a specialist they are required to share the information with the entire class. This involvement permits learners to stretch their learning boundaries and enrich their learning experiences. This process is conducted throughout the entire course since exchanges by e-mail normally require more time than direct contact.

POTENTIAL NEGATIVE IMPACTS

Nothing in this world is perfect. There are limitations on this design as with most things in life. Because of this, it is necessary to understand not only the strengths but also the weaknesses of the interactive online collaborative learning community design. Some of the potential negative impacts or weaknesses are discussed in the following sections.

Are Learners Ready?

Collaborative learning may not be new to most learners; however, their experiences and reactions vary widely. The main purpose of collaborative learning is to enrich learners' critical thinking, information exchange, and knowledge-generating processes and to attain rich interactive learning experiences. If learners do not see the value of collaborative learning, they will focus only on achievement and will not engage effectively in collaborative activities. The perception acquired by learners involved in collaborative learning is very critical and success depends upon a clear understanding of its purposes and values. The instructor must assist students in developing this positive perception before any collaborative learning activities can occur.

Time Intensive

Online collaborative learning is not as efficient as traditional face-to-face collaborative learning. Team communication by computer-mediated communication requires more time to achieve a consensus. There is the risk that a team may not be able to achieve some tasks if appropriate support is missing or too little time is allotted.

Intensive Monitoring

Instructors must monitor collaborative activities closely because online collaborative learning is a slow process. It demands more time and effort from instructors to ensure that all teams are making progress throughout the entire course. Again, good planning, organizing, and managing are critical.

Failure

With the absence of visual communication (facial expressions, body language, speaking tone), online collaborative learning may be more prone toward failure. Therefore, it is vital that any difficulties within teams are reported to the instructor early on so that teams do not become frustrated and fail to complete assignments.

CONCLUSIONS

Organization, management, and planning are required to engage students in interactive online learning through the integration of the online collaborative learning community design. Traditional face-to-face instruction does not adapt to the online learning environment. Online instructors and instructional designers should provide interactive learning conditions to maximize learning. Instructors should transfer the accountability for learning to learners and provide them with opportunities to negotiate when, where, how, and what they learn by applying computer technologies.

REFERENCES

Benbunan-Fich, R., & Hiltz, S. R. (1999). Educational applications of CMCS: Solving case studies through asynchronous learning networks. *Journal of Computer-Mediated Communication, 4*(3). Retrieved January 15, 2002, from http://www.ascusc. org/jcmc/vol4/issue3/benbunan-fich.html

Cooper, J., & Robinson, P. (1998). Small-group instruction in science, mathematics, engineering and technology (SMET) disciplines: A status report and an agenda for the future. *Journal of College Science Teaching, 27*(6), 383-388. Retrieved March 3, 2002, from http://www.csudh.edu/soe/cl_network/RTinCL.html

Eisenstadt, M. (1995). *The knowledge media generation.* Retrieved September 25, 2002, from http://kmi.open.ac.uk/kmi-misc/kmi-feature.html

Gerdy, K. B. (1998). If Socrates only knew: Expanding law class discourse. Paper presented at the annual conference for Law School Computing Online Conference. Retrieved March 6, 2002, from http://www.cali.org/conference/1998/postconf/thursday/ 25c4a/

Golub, J. (1988). *Focus on collaborative learning.* Urbana, IL: National Council of Teachers of English.

Gunawardena, C. N. (1995). Interaction–Affirmative (Opening Statement). *ICDE95: Debate on Interaction.* Retrieved July 21, 1998, from http://www.ualberta.ca/ ~tanderso/icde95/interaction_www/0009.html

Jarvenpaa, S. L., Knoll, K., & Leidner, D. E. (1998). Is anybody out there? Antecedents of trust in global virtual teams. *Journal of Management Information Systems, 14*(4), 29-64.

Johnson, D. W., Johnson, R. T., & Holubec, E. J. (1990). *Circles of learning: Cooperation in the classroom.* Edina, MN: Interaction Book Co.

Latham, G. P., & Locke, E. A. (1991). Self-regulation through goal setting. *Organizational Behavior and Human Decision Processes, 50*(2), 212-247.

Ocker, R. J., & Yaverbaum, G. (1999). Asynchronous computer-mediated communication versus face-to-face collaboration: Results on student learning, quality and satisfaction. *Group Decision and Negotiation, 8*, 427-440.

Panitz, T. (1996). *A definition of collaborative vs cooperative learning.* Retrieved March 18, 2002, from http://www.lgu.ac.uk/deliberations/collab.learning/panitz2. html

Scifres, E. L., Gundersen, D. E., & Behara, R. S. (1998). An empirical investigation of electronic groups in the classroom. *Journal of Education for Business, 73*(4), 247-250.

Slavin, R. E. (1991). Synthesis of research of cooperative learning. *Educational Leadership, 48*(5), 71-82.

Snow, C. C., Snell, S. A., & Davison, S. C. (1996). Use transnational teams to globalize your company. *Organizational Dynamics, 24*(4), 50-67.

Springer, L., Stanne, M. E., & Donovan, S. (1997). *Effects of small-group learning on undergraduates in science, mathematics, engineering, and technology: A meta-analysis.* Paper presented at the annual meeting of the Association for the Study of Higher Education. (ERIC Document Reproduction Service No. ED415814)

Stahl, R. J. (1994). The essential elements of cooperative learning in the classroom. *ERIC Digest.* Retrieved March 12, 2002, from http://www.ed.gov/databases/ERIC_Digests/ed370881.html (ERIC Document Reproduction Service No. ED370881)

Stahl, R. J., & VanSickle, R. L. (1992). *Cooperative learning in the social studies classroom: An introduction to social study* (Bulletin No. 87). Washington, DC: National Council for the Social Studies. (ERIC Document Reproduction Service No. ED361243)

Tu, C. H., & Corry, M. (2002). eLearning community. *The Quarterly Review of Distance Education, 3*(2), 207-218.

David Winograd

The Roles, Functions and Skills of Moderators of Online Educational Computer Conferences for Distance Education

SUMMARY. The success or failure of an asynchronous computer conference as part of a distance education course is largely dependent upon the abilities of the moderator of the conference. This paper discusses various skills and responsibilities of a moderator. It includes a discussion of ineffective moderation and how to avoid making common mistakes by examining skills used by effective moderators to enhance, enliven, and assist students to bring meaning to the discussion in an atmosphere of warmth and mutual support. *[Article copies available for a fee from The Haworth Document Delivery Service: 1-800-HAWORTH. E-mail address: <docdelivery@ haworthpress.com> Website: <http://www.HaworthPress.com> © 2003 by The Haworth Press, Inc. All rights reserved.]*

KEYWORDS. Moderator, facilitator, computer-mediated communication, online, conferencing, asynchronous, moderated, distance, discussion, moderation

DAVID WINOGRAD is Assistant Professor, Information and Communication Technology, State University of New York, College at Potsdam, Potsdam, NY 13662 (E-mail: winogrdm@potsdam.edu).

[Haworth co-indexing entry note]: "The Roles, Functions and Skills of Moderators of Online Educational Computer Conferences for Distance Education." Winograd, David. Co-published simultaneously in *Computers in the Schools* (The Haworth Press, Inc.) Vol. 20, No. 3, 2003, pp. 61-72; and: *Distance Education: What Works Well* (ed: Michael Corry, and Chih-Hsiung Tu) The Haworth Press, Inc., 2003, pp. 61-72. Single or multiple copies of this article are available for a fee from The Haworth Document Delivery Service [1-800-HAWORTH, 9:00 a.m. - 5:00 p.m. (EST). E-mail address: docdelivery@haworthpress.com].

It has been widely held that interaction is critical to learning and an essential part of the academic process (Berge, 1996; Kearsley, 1990; Parker, 1999; Phipps & Merisotis, 2000; Telg, 1990). Summers (1991) reasoned that without interaction teaching was reduced to "passing on knowledge as if it were dogmatic truth" (p. 14). This transferal model of learning eliminated any evaluation of the information transferred (Shale & Garrison, 1990a). Parker (1999) proposed that it is not sufficient for instruction to be transmitted linearly from instructor to student without interaction. "Today's distance education courses must authorize students to question their ideas and beliefs, thereby, encouraging provocative and interactive construction of personal knowledge" (p. 13). Peters (1999) concurred by stating, "If we take distance education seriously and understand it to be something more than the mere distribution of reading materials, we must provide sufficient opportunities for dialogues" (p. 13). A moderator of an asynchronous computer conference within a distance education course is a catalyst for interaction and, as such, bears careful consideration.

DEFINING MODERATORS

A moderator is crucial to the success of a computer conference. The position requires someone that is a veritable jack-of-all-trades (Rubin, 1996). McCreary (1990) likened the position of a moderator to the lead player in a jazz ensemble. At the start the players do not know exactly what roles they will play in relation to one another, or what their contribution might be. The moderator organizes and leads the players to create an ensemble and harmoniously arrive at a theme. An excellent definition of a moderator is found in *War and Peace* as Tolstoy described how Anna Pavlovna ran her salon:

> As the foreman of a spinning-mill when he has set the hands to work, goes round and notices, here a spindle that has stopped or there one that creaks or makes more noise than it should, and hastens to check the machine or set it in proper motion, so Anna Pavlovna moved about her drawing-room, approaching now a silent, now a too noisy group, and by a word or slight re-arrangement kept the conversation machine in steady, proper, and regular motion. (Tolstoy, 1930, pp. 11-12)

A moderator provides motivation and inertia to an asynchronous computer conference, encouraging interaction between participants while creating a supportive and comfortable environment for discussion.

ROLES OF A MODERATOR

In a survey of 156 moderators of online newsgroups, Collins and Berge (1997) found that they categorized their roles as follows:

1. Content filter (32%)–keeping a high signal/noise ratio, weeding out irrelevant material.
2. Firefighter (14%)–preventing flame wars and personal attacks.
3. Facilitator (12%)–keeping the conference focused on a mission.
4. Administrator (10%)–helping with technical problems and maintenance.
5. Editor (10%)–clarifying, asking for clarification, adding references, etc.
6. Promoter (7%)–generating discussion, noting threads of particular interest.
7. Expert (7%)–evaluating accuracy of posts, answering technical questions.
8. Helper (2%)–helping people with various needs.
9. Participant (2%)–just another member of the group.
10. Marketer (1%)–explaining the conference to potential members (p. 1).

IMPROPER MODERATION

When moderators are improperly trained or used in an online conference, it is inevitable that problems will occur. In a study using student moderators in an online class of preservice teachers, Cifuentes, Murphy, Segur, and Kodali (1997) reported that when teachers employed extremely tight controls, problems resulted. The moderators and students were constrained by being assigned all of the discussion topics, the length of time allowed for discussion, the number of messages that the students were required to contribute for credit, and the groupings of the students. The moderators were given little freedom throughout the conference. The results were that some students refused to participate or post messages merely to fulfill minimum course requirements. A number of students were hostile to the teacher and other students, both in lab sections and in the computer conference. Moderators and students were confused over the difference between e-mail and computer conferencing. In one case, moderators had to be changed three times during one semester. This led to the students becoming discouraged over the lack of leadership. Moderators, especially if moderation is done by students, need a good deal of autonomy. This often includes being able to determine discussion topics and having the freedom to infuse the conference with their unique personalities. Allowing moderators autonomy brings a feeling of "ownership" of the discussion, which is quite motivating.

Moderators need to give explicit direction to their groups. It has been known to happen that students post a message and then leave the conference or drop out of the course due to poor moderation. In one case, when later asked why the course was dropped, the student explained that after she posted her introductory message, she expected the group to comment on what she had said. When this failed to happen, she became disheartened and left the group (Palloff & Pratt, 1999).

A hands-off approach to moderation has proven to be detrimental to groups both online and off. Students excited over the prospect of using a new technology often get frustrated when they wait days for responses. This may lead to group members posting off-topic, or submitting stiff canned-sounding messages that do not further the current conversation (Eastmond, 1995). In a study of learning teams in face-to-face groups at Case Western Reserve University, it was found that, when a facilitator assumed a premeditated distant approach of not intervening in group leadership or decision making, group members became deadlocked over issues intended to be discussed and agreed upon; they became divisive, attacking the course, and splintered into factions (McMillen, White, & McKee, 1994).

FUNCTIONS OF A SUCCESSFUL MODERATOR

There has been a large body of research, case studies, and anecdotal reports written over the last decade specifically detailing what moderators have done to lead successful academic conferences. Mason (1991) divided the work of a moderator into tasks divided between organizational, social, and intellectual concerns. Berge (1995) added a technical category to the list. The collected body of work displays a remarkable commonality of findings.

Organizational Functions of a Moderator

This set of functions is concerned with getting a conference established and continuing with functions that would help the conference run smoothly. This list starts with items that are important during the first few weeks of the conference when problems are inevitable and solutions must quickly be found.

1. Help individuals get started (Carlson, 1989).
2. Provide for adequate technical support (Eastmond, 1995; Hiemstra, 1992; Rohfeld & Hiemstra, 1995).
3. Plan time to help participants with the software (Berge, 1995; Cifuentes et al., 1997; Hiemstra, 1992).
4. Avoid frustrating procedural trivia (Paulsen, 1995).
5. Do not overload with too much information (Berge, 1995; Harasim, Hiltz, Teles, & Turoff, 1995; Paulsen, 1995).
6. Contract for a minimum level of participation (Cifuentes et al., 1997; Eastmond, 1995; Harasim et al., 1995; Paulsen, 1995; Rohfeld & Hiemstra, 1995).
7. Be patient (Berge, 1995; Rezabek, 1993; Rheingold, 1998).
8. Be flexible (Berge, 1995; Brochet, 1989; Harasim et al., 1995; Rohfeld & Hiemstra, 1995).

The next organizationally oriented functions give students a sense of how the conference is run. These functions establish a few basic boundaries and housekeeping procedures.

9. Set agendas (Feenberg, 1989).
10. Give explicit directions (Eastmond, 1995; Harasim et al., 1995).
11. Create rules and standards for appropriate online behavior (Harasim et al., 1995).
12. Be clear and unequivocal (Berge, 1995; Harasim et al., 1995; Paulsen, 1995).
13. Do not change established rules (Rheingold, 1998).
14. Spur participation (Berge, 1995; Carlson, 1989; Eastmond, 1992; Feenberg, 1989; Green, 1998; Harasim et al., 1995).
15. Move misplaced messages (Berge, 1995; Harasim et al., 1995; Paulsen, 1995).
16. Handle and redirect tangents (Berge, 1995; Paulsen, 1995).
17. End each topic decisively (Berge, 1995; Paulsen, 1995).

The last set of organizationally based rules deals with potential problems that if not identified can damage the sense of equality between participants or result in the conference becoming stale and losing its vitality.

18. Use e-mail to put out flames and soothe hurt feelings (Berge, 1995; Hoag, Williams, & Fox, 1996).
19. Do not let the group lose sight of its objectives (Green, 1998).
20. Do not allow the more verbal members to dominate the group (Harasim et al., 1995; Hoag et al., 1996; Paulsen, 1995).
21. Retire topics according to a predetermined plan (Rheingold, 1998).
22. Communicate via e-mail with the promising and the troublemakers (Berge, 1995).
23. Use authority wisely (Rheingold, 1998).

Social Functions of a Moderator

These socially oriented functions are meant to foster the kindling that can ignite a community. Rheingold (1998) contended that "communities can't be manufactured, but you can design the conditions under which they are most likely to emerge, and encourage their growth when they do" (p. 2). In an educationally oriented computer conference, although it is not a given that community will occur, the chances are quite good because the community derives a good deal of its purpose, importance, and identity from the context of the course it supports. Social functions of moderators include the following:

1. Welcome participants (Green, 1998; Gunawardena, 1995; Hoag et al., 1996; Rheingold, 1998).

2. Realize that first reactions are critical; praise and mention people by name (Green, 1998; Rheingold, 1998).
3. Create a context conducive to creativity and positive self-esteem by providing timely positive feedback (Carlson, 1989; Green, 1998; Hoag et al., 1996; Kerr, 1986).
4. Use an icebreaker activity at the start of the conference (Green, 1998; Harasim et al., 1995; Herring & Smaldino, 1998).
5. Establish trust early (Eastmond, 1995; Rheingold, 1998).
6. Reinforce good behavior with politeness (Paulsen, 1995).
7. Construct a friendly and supportive atmosphere with as much informality as possible (Collins & Berge, 1996; Green, 1998; Gunawardena, 1995; Rohfeld & Hiemstra, 1995).
8. Tactfully ask for changes in questionable behavior (Paulsen, 1995).
9. Request *metacommunication*, which is communication about communication, by asking for the restatement of ideas that might be confusing or unclear (Berge, 1995; Feenberg, 1989; Harasim et al., 1995; Paulsen, 1995).
10. Plan for and facilitate interaction (Berge, 1995; Little, 1995).
11. Be mindful of humor and sarcasm that often do not translate (Berge, 1995; Green, 1998).
12. Encourage users to e-mail to each other to further interaction (Paulsen, 1995; Rheingold, 1998).
13. Communicate a sense of enthusiasm and zest (Rezabek, 1993; Rohfeld & Hiemstra, 1995).
14. Respond to messages promptly (Berge, 1995; Eastmond, 1995; Harasim et al., 1995; Hoag et al., 1996; Paulsen, 1995).
15. Request meta-comments to find and remediate potential problems, e.g., "How did you feel about that?" (Collins & Berge, 1996; Feenberg, 1989; Paulsen, 1995).

Intellectual Functions of a Moderator

These functions are directed toward the content of the course. They facilitate and clarify learning.

1. Model the intellectual tone for the conference (Bull, Harris, & Drucker, 1992; Hiemstra, 1992). This cannot be stressed highly enough. Novice users of computer conferencing want to know exactly what is expected of them and modeling the expected discourse with a well-crafted welcome message at the start of a conference, goes a long way toward relieving the uncertainty of writing and posting messages.
2. Require that messages be relevant (Cifuentes et al., 1997; Eastmond & Ziegahn, 1995; Paulsen, 1995).
3. Make sure that messages are substantial. It is not enough for participants to post a line or two agreeing or disagreeing with a previous posi-

tion. Each message must further the discussion by bringing up new points or taking the discussion in new directions.

4. Summarize discussions (Davis & Brewer, 1997; Eastmond, 1992; Green, 1998; Paulsen, 1995).
5. Present conflicting opinions (Berge, 1995; Paulsen, 1995).
6. Do not lecture (Berge, 1995; Collins & Berge, 1996; Harasim et al., 1995; Paulsen, 1995).
7. Periodically bring in new material to freshen up the discussion (Carlson, 1989; Hoag et al., 1996).
8. Provoke and instigate controversy (Paulsen, 1995).
9. Replace missing cues by contextualizing, thus establishing general topicality.
10. Weave salient points together using metacommunication. If not done by a moderator, often important larger concepts will be lost (Berge, 1995; Carlson, 1989; Feenberg, 1989; Green, 1998; Harasim et al., 1995; Hiemstra, 1992; Mason, 1991; Murphy, Cifuentes, Yakimovicz, Segur, Mahoney, & Kodali, 1996; Paulsen, 1995; Rohfeld & Hiemstra, 1995).

WEAVING

Weaving was the most repeated concept in the literature of online conference moderating. In face-to-face discourse the metacommunication engaged in is mainly accomplished through body language. If someone seems bored or distracted when another is speaking, the speaker can easily pick up the message by observing the social cue of the fidgeting listener. Online, the only cue that can be sent is silence, which hardly communicates anything at all, and what it does communicate is ambiguous. Weaving is explicit metacommunication relating to an online discussion. It summarizes the discussion and extracts its major themes and disagreements to clarify a discussion that has gone off in directions that people are having trouble following (Feenberg, 1989). Weaving is a skill that a good moderator learns by being aware that a discussion, over time, is not necessarily linear. It takes practice to start seeing things that appear out of order as a coherent discussion, and the moderator, at least once a week, can assist the group by weaving together recently posted ideas salient to the discussion.

MODERATORS
AND THE CONFERENCING ENVIRONMENT

To encourage interaction and collaboration, a moderator must craft an environment conducive to learning. A computer conference must be tightly and meaningfully integrated into the course (Collins & Berge, 1996). Conferences should be started with introductions and social interaction (Gunawardena, 1995; Palloff & Pratt, 1999). There are many ways that an appropriate environment can be constructed. A moderator should find multiple methods of creating salience, such as arranging comfortable electronic spaces for purely social purposes (Bull et al., 1992). A comfortable and informal setting should be encouraged with a number of topics having to do with social issues (Rohfeld & Hiemstra, 1995).

Some conferences contain energetic participation, while others seemingly designed to discuss equally interesting and relevant topics fail miserably with only minor flurries of activity, affording little value to the student. Therefore, a flexible approach to moderation is key to building an energetic and productive environment (Brochet, 1989). Creating a friendly environment for learning, according to Mason (1991), is essential. A moderator should send welcome messages and encourage participation, but also provide plenty of feedback to the students. When doing this, it is quite important to use a friendly and personal tone. Welcome messages should convey that each group member is an important and valued member of the community and all contributions, given the constraints of the particular conference, are critical to the success of the conference. Welcome messages should also contain a number of open-ended questions designed to get the discussion started.

CONTRACTING FOR PARTICIPATION

Saba and Shearer (1994) maintained that, in a distance education course, structure is in opposition to dialogue. When one element is increased, it causes an inverse reaction in the other. This may have been the case when, as in their study, communication between the teacher and student was the only sort of interaction studied, but, when interaction between learners is taken into account, Vrasidas and McIsaac (1999) found that structure tends to increase interaction; therefore, creating structure is one of the main tasks of a moderator.

In a conference where posting is voluntary, it is common for only about 20% of the participants to post even one message (Green, 1998; Rubin, 1996). It has been posed that the proper size of a group should be the same size as is found in a classroom, around 25 members (Green, 1998; Wells, 1992). In very small conferences of under 8 people, it is difficult to spark discussion because everyone feels that he/she must constantly perform. Seeing both sides of the problem, it is proposed that the correct size for a group is between 10 to 13 participants (Cifuentes et al., 1997) and that full participation be required. In a conference with little participation, Hacker and Wignall (1997) observed that participation of students with low degrees of computer experience declined significantly over time. Therefore, a minimum level of participation should be mandated at the start of the conference. This can be accomplished either by establishing a written or verbal contract between the moderator or teacher and the students (Rohfeld & Hiemstra, 1995). Eastmond and Ziegahn (1995) maintained that along with mandating a certain number of messages per week, there should be standards established for the quality and relevance of the messages. They suggested that participation account for 30% of the course grade. It has also been proposed that the amount and quality of participation should be able to raise or lower assessment by a full letter grade (Cifuentes et al., 1997). Many conferences take time to get established and spark general interest to the extent that the members need no incentive to post messages; therefore, it is important to establish a mandate to give the conference time to come into its own.

CONCLUSION

Trained and prepared moderators are not only important to the success of a computer conference but more importantly are crucial to the success of distance education courses. Without the direction and resulting interaction between moderator and learner and learner and learner, a distance education course often reduces to nothing more than a correspondence course using the Internet instead of stamp, with students reading page after page of text but not having a chance to discuss course material with their peers. Interaction, planned and motivated by a moderator, brings an added dimension to content as students offer their points of view and, in an organized manner, come to a deeper meaning of the content of the course.

Moderators need to be prepared and trained to provide support in organizational, social, and intellectual aspects of conferencing, realizing that each of the three are important to the well-being of the conference. A successful computer conference doesn't just happen. It is, in large part, due to the planning, created structure, and inherent motivation of a moderator skilled in a broad knowledge of the craft.

REFERENCES

Berge, Z. L. (1995). Facilitating computer conferencing: Recommendations from the field. *Educational Technology, 35*(1), 22-30.

Berge, Z. L. (1996). Where interaction intersects time. *MC Journal: The Journal of Academic Media Librarianship, 4*(1), 69-83.

Brochet, M. G. (1989). Effective moderation of computer conferences: Notes and suggestions. In M. G. Brochet (Ed.), *Moderating conferences* (pp. 6.01-08). Guelph, Ontario: University of Guelph.

Bull, G., Harris, J., & Drucker, D. (1992). Building an electronic culture: The academic village at Virginia. In M. D. Waggoner (Ed.), *Empowering networks: Computer conferencing in education* (pp. 35-53). Englewood Cliffs, NJ: Educational Technology Publications.

Carlson, L. (1989). Effective moderation of computer conferences: Hints for moderators. In M. G. Brochet (Ed.), *Moderating conferences* (pp. 6.10-16.13). Guelph, Ontario: University of Guelph.

Cifuentes, L., Murphy, K., Segur, R., & Kodali, S. (1997). Design considerations for computer conferencing. *The Journal of Research and Computing, 302*(2), 177-201.

Collins, M. P., & Berge, Z. L. (1996). *Facilitating interaction in computer mediated online courses.* [On-line]. Retrieved June 17, 1996, from http://star.ucc.nau.edu/~mauri/moderate/flcc.html

Collins, M. P., & Berge, Z. L. (1997, March 24-28). *Moderating online electronic discussion groups.* Paper presented at the American Educational Research Association, Chicago.

Davis, B. H., & Brewer, J. P. (1997). *Electronic discourse: Linguistic individuals in virtual space.* Albany: State University of New York Press.

Eastmond, D. V. (1992). Effective facilitation of computer conferencing. *Continuing Higher Education Review, 56*(1-2), 23-34.

Eastmond, D. V. (1995). *Alone but together: Adult distance study through computer conferencing.* Cresskill: Hampton Press.

Eastmond, D. V., & Ziegahn, L. (1995). Instructional design for the online classroom. In Z. L. Berge & M. P. Collins (Eds.), *Computer mediated communication and the online classroom: Distance education* (Vol. 3, pp. 59-80). Cresskill, NJ: Hampton Press.

Feenberg, A. (1989). The written word: On the theory and practice of computer conferencing. In R. Mason & A. R. Kaye (Eds.), *Mindweave: Communications, computers, and distance education* (pp. 22-39). Oxford: Pergamon Press.

Green, L. (1998). *Playing croquet with flamingos: A guide to moderating online conferences* (Guide). Quebec, Canada: Office of Learning Technologies, Human Resources Department.

Gunawardena, C. N. (1995). Social presence theory and implications for interactive and collaborative learning in computer conferences community shared experience moderators. *International Journal of Educational Telecommunication, 1*(2/3), 147-166.

Hacker, K. L., & Wignall, D. L. (1997). Issues in predicting user acceptance of computer-mediated communication (CMC) in inter-university classroom discussion as an alternative to face-to-face interaction. *Communication Reports, 10*(1), 107-114.

Harasim, L., Hiltz, S. R., Teles, L., & Turoff, M. (1995). *Learning networks: A field guide to teaching and learning networks.* Cambridge: The MIT Press.

Herring, M. C., & Smaldino, S. E. (1998). *Planning for interactive distance education: A handbook.* Washington, DC: Association for Educational Communications and Technology.

Hiemstra, R. (1992). Computerized distance education: The role for facilitators. *The MPAEA Journal of Adult Education, 22*(2), 11-23.

Hoag, J. D., Williams, G. A., & Fox, M. (1996, January). *The WELL host manual.* [Online]. Retrieved May 12, 1997, from http://www.well.com/user/confteam/hostmanual/

Kearsley, G. (1990). Designing educational software for international use. *Journal of Research on Computing in Education, 23*(2), 242-249.

Kerr, E. (1986). Electronic leadership: A guide to moderating online conferences. *IEEE Transactions on professional communication. PC, 29*(1), 12-18.

Little, J. K. (1995). *The distance learning classroom: Identifying a process for facilitating interaction (faculty training).* Unpublished Doctoral Dissertation, University of Tennessee, Knoxville.

Mason, R. (1991). Moderating educational computer conferencing: *DEOSNEWS, 1*(19) (Vol. 1). Archived as DEOSNEWS 91-00011 on LISTSERV@PSVUM.

McCreary, E. (1990). Three behavioral models for computer-mediated communication. In L. Harasim (Ed.), *Online education: Perspectives in a new environment.* New York: Praeger.

McMillen, C., White, J., & McKee, A. (1994). Assessing managerial skills in a social context. *Journal of Management Education, 18*(2), 162-185.

Murphy, K. L., Cifuentes, L., Yakimovicz, A. D., Segur, R., Mahoney, S. E., & Kodali, S. (1996). Students assume the mantle of moderating computer conferences: A case study. *The American Journal of Distance Education, 10*(3), 20-36.

Palloff, I. M., & Pratt, K. (1999). *Building learning communities in cyberspace: Effective strategies for the online classroom.* San Francisco: Jossey-Bass.

Parker, A. (1999, Autumn/Winter). Interaction in distance education: The critical conversation. *Educational Technology Review,* 13-17.

Paulsen, M. F. (1995). Moderating educational computer conferences. In Z. L. Berge & M. P. Collins (Eds.), *Computer mediated communication and the online classroom: Distance learning* (Vol. 3, pp. 81-89). Cresskill, NJ: Hampton Press.

Peters, O. (1999). *Teaching and learning in distance education: Analysis and interpretation from an international perspective.* London: Kogan Page Limited.

Phipps, R., & Merisotis, J. (2000). *Quality on the line: Benchmarks for success in Internet-based distance education.* Washington, DC: The Institute for Higher Education Policy.

Rezabek, L. L. (1993, June 25-29). *Teaching with distance delivery systems: Strategies from alpha to omega.* Paper presented at the Verbo-Visual Literacy: Understanding and Applying New Educational Communication Media Technologies. Selected Readings from the Symposium of the International Visual Literacy Association, Delphi, Greece.

Rheingold, H. (1998). *The art of hosting good conversation online.* [Online]. Retrieved April 1, 1998, from http://www.rheingold.com/texts/artonlinehost.html

Rohfeld, R. W., & Hiemstra, R. (1995). Moderating discussions in the electronic classroom. In Z. L. Berge & M. P. Collins (Eds.), *Computer mediated communication and the online classroom: Distance learning* (Vol. 3, pp. 91-104). Cresskill, NJ: Hampton Press.

Rubin, E. (1996, April). *The ups and downs of running a listserv-based computer conference.* Retrieved May 22, 1999, from http://star.ucc.nau.edu/~mauri/moderate/rubin.html#plans

Saba, F., & Shearer, R. L. (1994). Verifying key theoretical concepts in a dynamic model of distance education. *The American Journal of Distance Education, 8*(1), 36-57.

Shale, D., & Garrison, D. R. (1990). Education and communication. In D. Shale & D. R. Garrison (Eds.), *Education at a distance: From issues to practice* (pp. 23-39). Malabar, FL: Robert E. Krieger.

Summers, J. (1991). Effect of interactivity upon student achievement completion intervals and affective perceptions. *Journal of Educational Technology Systems, 19*(1), 53-57.

Telg, R. (1990). Introduction. In D. Shale & D. R. Garrison (Eds.), *Education at a distance: From issues to practice* (pp. 1-6). Malabar, FL: Robert E. Krieger.

Tolstoy, L. (1930). *War and peace* (L. Maude & A. Maude, Trans.) (Vol. 1). London: Oxford University Press.

Vrasidas, C., & McIsaac, M. (1999). Factors influencing interaction in an online course. *The American Journal of Distance Education, 13*(3), 22-36.

Wells, R. (1992). Computer-mediated communication for distance education: An international review of design teaching and institutional issues. *The American Center for the Study of Distance Education.*

Atsusi Hirumi

Get a Life:
Six Tactics for Optimizing
Time Spent Online

SUMMARY. A frequent concern raised by distance educators is that e-learning takes more time to facilitate than traditional classroom instruction. The simple fact that it takes more time to read and write than to speak and listen warrants consideration. To establish viable e-learning programs, we need to optimize the amount of time educators spend online. This article posits five tactics for optimizing time spent facilitating the e-learning process and one tactic for optimizing time spent developing e-learning materials. Together, the tactics applied within the context of an overall systematic instructional design process yield replicable results. The investment in systematic design is thought worthwhile because the materials are reusable and allow instructors to focus their attention on facilitating, rather than directing and clarifying, the e-learning process. *[Article copies available for a fee from The Haworth Document Delivery Service: 1-800-HAWORTH. E-mail address: <docdelivery@haworthpress.com> Website: <http://www.HaworthPress.com> © 2003 by The Haworth Press, Inc. All rights reserved.]*

ATSUSI HIRUMI is Assistant Professor and Program Chair, Instructional Technology Department, University of Houston–Clear Lake, Houston, TX 77058 (E-mail: hirumi@cl.uh.edu).

[Haworth co-indexing entry note]: "Get a Life: Six Tactics for Optimizing Time Spent Online." Hirumi, Atsusi. Co-published simultaneously in *Computers in the Schools* (The Haworth Press, Inc.) Vol. 20, No. 3, 2003, pp. 73-101; and: *Distance Education: What Works Well* (ed: Michael Corry, and Chih-Hsiung Tu) The Haworth Press, Inc., 2003, pp. 73-101. Single or multiple copies of this article are available for a fee from The Haworth Document Delivery Service [1-800-HAWORTH, 9:00 a.m. - 5:00 p.m. (EST). E-mail address: docdelivery@haworthpress.com].

KEYWORDS. E-learning, Web-based instruction, interactivity, online learning, Web-based education, systematic design

Do you feel that e-learning takes too much time: too much time to design high-quality e-learning materials and too much time to manage the e-learning process? Modern e-learning management systems (LMS), such as CourseInfo, WebCT, Centra, and WebEx, make it easier to facilitate telecommunications and to post educational materials online. However, LMSs neither transform traditional teaching materials into effective e-learning resources, nor prevent educators from being inundated by e-mail and bulletin board postings. Ease of use does not necessarily translate into the development of innovative environments that use the potential of emerging technologies to stimulate collaborative and individual learning. On the contrary, an LMS can lead to a false sense of efficiency and an increased workload.

For teachers, ease of use may mean that the LMS organizes information in familiar ways, using terms and features common in traditional classroom settings. Administrators may think that with an LMS, a user's manual, and some training, educators should be able to author marketable e-learning materials and offer meaningful e-learning experiences with little to no additional time or resources. Under such conditions, educators have little choice but to do what they know best. In most cases, that means applying teacher-directed instructional methods and materials. The problem is that traditional classroom teaching methods and materials are often insufficient or inappropriate for facilitating e-learning.

Lecture notes, overhead transparencies (converted into PowerPoint slides), handouts, and course syllabi are based on an oral teaching tradition. They rely heavily on an instructor and students to *speak* and *listen* to each other to convey information, clarify expectations, define procedures, explain requirements, establish policies, complete assignments, and otherwise derive meaning from and construct knowledge of the subject matter in real time. Simply translating traditional classroom materials into an electronic format does not ensure that essential interactions will occur.

During e-learning, opportunities for synchronous interactions are relatively limited. Most communications occur asynchronously through *reading* and *writing*. Key interactions that occur verbally and spontaneously in traditional classroom settings must be written and planned as an integral part of e-learning. The effort necessary to generate, disseminate, read, interpret, and otherwise manage written communications and inadequate course design are believed to be the two primary reasons why it takes so much time to teach online.

So what can educators do to optimize time spent online? If educators are given access or time to generate quality e-learning materials, will it still take more time to facilitate and manage e-learning than traditional classroom instruction? What should educators do with limited time and resources? This paper explores these questions and posits several potential answers. Specifically, I describe five tactics for optimizing time spent facilitating the e-learning process and one tactic for optimizing time spent producing e-learning materials. Even with such tactics, it is important to recognize that the design and development of high quality instructional materials take considerable time and effort (for any learning environment). I conclude by discussing key factors to consider when determining if the tactics yield a sufficient return on investment.

SIX OPTIMIZING TACTICS

Align and Publish Objectives and Assessments

Learning objectives and student assessments are well-known components of the instructional process. Few, however, seem to approach these two vital elements in a systematic fashion. As a student, have you ever taken a test and wondered where some of the questions came from? Have you ever doubted what would be on a test or what the teacher was looking for in a class project or assignment? Have you ever spent a lot of time and effort on an assignment only to receive a bad grade, not because you didn't have the skills or knowledge, but because you just did not know what the instructor wanted? Teachers often spend time before, during, or after class clarifying expectations. Questions such as "Is this what you want?" and "What will be on the test?" are common in traditional classroom settings. During e-learning, such questions can easily overwhelm distance educators. Instructors may have to spend considerable time online clarifying expectations if (a) the objectives and performance criteria are not explicit, and (b) the behaviors specified in course objectives or practiced in class do not match the behaviors required to successfully complete assignments and examinations.

The alignment of objectives and assessment criteria is fundamental to high-quality instruction (Berge, 2002; Dick, Carey, & Carey, 2001). To optimize learning, students should be informed of what they are expected to know and be able to do, and they should be evaluated using assessment items and published performance criteria that match the behaviors specified in the objectives. If an objective states that students will be able to *list* key concepts, assessments should ask students to *list* key concepts. If an objective states that learners will be able to *compare* cases, assessment should ask learners to *compare* cases.

In traditional classroom settings, educators can readily address questions regarding unclear or contradictory expectations. During e-learning, the communications necessary to clarify misaligned or poorly communicated objectives and criteria can take a lot of time, particularly if students submit unsatisfactory assignments that require considerable feedback and remediation. Worse yet, incongruent instructional elements may result in significant misunderstandings that are left unattended because learners are too confused or otherwise reluctant to initiate communications with the instructor. If the elements are aligned, you can optimize time online by preventing unnecessary logistical questions, by referring learners to published objectives and criteria if asked to clarify expectations, and by using published criteria to prepare timely and detailed feedback.

The development of a design evaluation chart can help ensure alignment between objectives and assessments. Table 1 depicts a two-column chart prepared for an instructional unit on criterion-referenced testing. Column one lists the objectives that are to be addressed by the unit. Column two specifies the assessment item(s) or assessment criteria that are to assess learners' achievement of the objectives. Alignment is achieved by matching the behaviors specified in each column. Note that to limit the size of Table 1 for publication only a limited set of objectives related to the unit is depicted.

Column two indicates that three types of assessments are to measure achievement of the specified unit objectives. A portfolio assessment rubric is to assess learner achievement of the terminal objective. A conventional multiple-choice test and a product checklist are to measure learners' achievement of the enabling objectives. Note that the assessment items and performance criteria listed in column two match the behaviors specified in the corresponding learning objectives in column one.

Of course, alignment is only useful if the objectives are valid. Before you begin aligning elements, ask yourself, "What is the course supposed to do?" List the learning goals and objectives for the entire course and assure that they are appropriate and are written in clear and measurable terms. Use the development of an e-learning course as an opportunity to reassess your goals and objectives. If you are unsure or do not have clearly defined objectives, consider some form of task analysis (cf., Jonassen, Tessmer, & Hannum, 1999) to identify essential skills and knowledge. Then generate, cluster, and sequence objectives into instructional units based on your analysis and prepare a design evaluation chart to align assessment criteria and items with the objectives.

Align Instructional Events to Support Objectives and Assessments

To facilitate e-learning, assignments and activities (i.e., instructional events) should also be aligned to support the achievement of specified objectives (Berge, 2002; Smith & Ragan, 1999). Students should be given opportunities to practice and otherwise develop the skills and knowledge specified in course and lesson objectives. To align instructional events with learning objectives, classify targeted objectives according to a particular learning taxonomy (e.g., Gagné, 1977). Then apply the assignments, activities, and instructional events that have been found to facilitate achievement of the desired outcomes. The methods used to teach concepts should differ from the methods used to teach a

TABLE 1. Sample Design Evaluation Chart for Instructional Unit on Criterion-Referenced Testing

Objective	Assessment Item

1. Given a set of instructional objectives, generate conventional and/or performance-based criterion-referenced tests that are congruent with targeted goals: learner, context, and published assessment criteria.	Descriptors for exemplary performance level for assessment rubric will be used to evaluate criterion-referenced test instruments.
	1. Goal-Centered Criteria
	  a. Matches behavior, including the action and concepts, prescribed in objectives.
	  b. Meets conditions specified in the objectives.
	2. Learner-Centered Criteria
	  a. Tailored to learners in terms of vocabulary, language levels, developmental levels, motivational and interest levels, experiences, backgrounds and special needs.
	  b. Free of gender, ethnic, or cultural biases.
	3. Context-Centered Criteria
	  a. Realistic or authentic to actual performance setting as possible.
	  b. Feasible and suited to resources available in learning setting.
	4. Assessment-Centered Criteria (for conventional test items)
	  a. Applies correct grammar, spelling, and punctuation.
	  b. Stem clearly formulates problem.
	  c. Stem contains task and most information, keeping answers/options short.
	  d. Stem includes only required information and is written in clear, positive manner.
	  e. Includes only one correct, defensible, best answer. Foils are plausible and do not contain unintentional clues.

2. Given a set of instructional situations, recognize when learner assessments are generated during systematic design process.	1. Learner assessments are created after _____ during the _____ phase of the systematic design process.
	  (a) establishing instructional strategy, design
	  (b) defining objectives, design
	  (c) defining objectives, development
	  (d) conducting goal analysis, analysis
	  (e) selecting media, development

3. Given a set of instructional situations, recall purposes of criterion-referenced testing (CRT).	1. Criterion-referenced tests can be used to measure students' entry-level behaviors.
	  a. true
	  b. false
	2. Criterion-referenced tests can be used to monitor students' progress toward learning objectives.
	  a. true
	  b. false

TABLE 1 (continued)

Objective	Assessment Item
4. Given a set of instructional situations, distinguish two forms of CRT.	1. The two basic forms of criterion-referenced tests are conventional and _____. a. norm-referenced b. fill-in-the-blank c. product checklists d. portfolio assessments e. performance-based assessments
5. Given a set of instructional situations, identify criteria for generating quality conventional assessment items.	1. An important goal-centered criterion for generating quality assessment instruments is that the items: a. match the behavior prescribed in objectives. b. are tailored to learners in terms of vocabulary and language. c. are realistic to actual performance setting. d. apply correct grammar. e. are performance-based assessments. 2. An important assessment-centered criterion for generating quality conventional test items is that the foils: (a) contain most of the information. (b) include only required information. (c) meet the conditions specified in the objectives. (d) are all plausible but consist of one best answer. (e) clearly formulate the problem.
6. Given a set of instructional situations, contrast conventional and performance-based assessments.	1. In contrast to conventional CRT, performance-based CRT: a. are used to sort and rank students. b. are one dimensional and episodic. c. measure students' acquisition of skills and knowledge. d. present explicit and published performance criteria. e. contain criteria that are prescribed by the instructor.
7. Given the results of a goal and subordinate skills analysis and a set of objectives, generate and align assessment items by generating a design evaluation chart.	1. Product checklist items with two possible levels of performance: (a) yes, and (b) no, and an opportunity to comment. a. assessment method clearly defined and appropriate for context and objectives. b. evaluation chart properly formatted. c. specified skills consistent with those identified in goal and subordinate skills analyses. d. objectives consistent with specified skills. e. assessment items congruent with objectives.

procedure that, in turn, should differ from the methods to teach complex problem solving, and so on. Smith and Ragan (1999) classify alternative instructional events that have been found to facilitate achievement of various learning outcomes (Table 2). Use the table to assure that you are using appropriate instructional events to facilitate e-learning and promote the achievement of targeted objectives. If an instructional unit addresses a range of learning objectives, place emphasis on the terminal objective (or the primary targeted learning outcome) when selecting an appropriate set of instructional events.

Adding a column to the design evaluation chart depicted in Table 1 will help ensure alignment between objectives, assessments, and instructional events (Table 3).

Column three describes the instructional events that will be used to help learners achieve the specified objectives. Again, alignment is achieved by matching the behaviors specified in each column. Column 3 notes that the learners are to generate criterion-referenced tests and complete reading assignments, a quiz, and a performance checklist to achieve the enabling and terminal objectives. In addition, grounded instructional events, or activities "rooted in established theory and research in human learning" (Hannifin, Hannifin, Land & Oliver, 1997, p. 102) are planned to facilitate e-learning. In this particular case, grounded events associated with the development of problem-solving skills (i.e., presentation of problem, discussion of problem space, identification of relevant principles and practice) are to be integrated within the unit. Note that to limit the size of Table 3 for publication only a limited set of objectives and assessments related to the unit is depicted.

Failure to align instructional events with specified learning objectives may result in insufficient or inappropriate learning. Students may find it difficult to successfully complete assignments and exams that, in turn, may require considerable feedback and remediation. The alignment of grounded instructional events is fundamental to high-quality instruction and particularly important to e-learning because the instructor may not be readily available nor have the time necessary to correct flaws in design. For further details on the design and sequencing of instructional events to formulate a comprehensive e-learning strategy, refer to Hirumi (2002a).

Analyze and Balance Interactions

Web courses that contain many interactions can be more complicated to complete than relatively linear programs (Gilbert & Moore, 1998). For novice distance learners, such complexity may lead to feelings of helplessness and confusion and eventually cause one to drop out. Dissatisfaction may also occur if learners perceive online interactions as meaningless busy work. Even experienced distance learners may find that the overuse or misuse of interactions results in frustration, boredom, and cognitive overload (Berge, 1999). Too many interactions may also overwhelm the instructor. A common concern ex-

TABLE 2. Grounded Instructional Events

Outcome	Grounded Events

1. **Verbal Information**
 	
Names, labels, facts, or a collection of propositions
	1. Associational Techniques
	  a. *Mnemonic & metaphoric devices*
	  b. *Instructor- or learner-generated images* (e.g., graphs) *and rehearsal* (e.g., drill and practice)
	2. Organizational Techniques
	  a. *Clustering and chunking into categories* (e.g., periodic table)
	  b. *Expository and narrative structures* (e.g., chronologies, cause and effect, problem solutions, contrasts)
	  c. *Graphic and advanced organizers* (e.g., concept tree or information linking new to prior knowledge)
	3. Elaboration Techniques
	  a. *Write meaningful sentences* (e.g., sentences using elements of periodic table)
	  b. *Devise rule* (e.g., describe why elements are organized in rows and columns)

2. **Concepts** Specific objects, symbols, or events, grouped on the basis of shared characteristics and which can be referenced by a particular name or symbol	1. *Inquiry approach* (e.g., exploratory learning beginning with examples and non-examples) 2. *Expository approach* (typically begins with an explanation of a concept and its key attributes) 3. *Attribute isolation* (points out the critical attributes of a concept) 4. *Concept trees* (graphic representations that illustrate subordinate and superordinate concepts) 5. *Analogies* (supplied by instructor or generated by learners) *and mnemonics* 6. *Imagery* (a mental image of concrete concepts, such as pictures, graphs, tables, and maps)
3. **Rules** Relational rules or principals and procedural rules or procedures	1. Learn to *determine if the procedure is required.* 2. Learn to *list the steps in a procedure.* 3. Learn to *complete the steps in a procedure.* 4. Learn to *elaborate sequence*, starting with simple epitome to more complex versions of same rule. 5. Learn to *check appropriateness of completed procedure.*

Outcome	Grounded Events
4. Problem Solving Learned principles, procedures, verbal information and cognitive strategies combined in a unique way within a domain to solve original problems	1. *Present problem* (Case studies, simulations, limiting the number of rules that must be used.) 2. *Discuss problem space* (Review directions and information about desired goal state. Define relationship between variables in current and goal state. Analyze relationships and discern patterns. Define knowns and unknowns. Determine information requirements. Break down problem into intermediate states.) 3. *Identify appropriate principles* (Guide questions or direct statements on how to select and apply appropriate principles.) 4. *Practice* (Present multiple representations of the problem. Recommend techniques for limiting alternative approaches to problem resolution. Provide clues about solution or intermediate solutions. Recommend strategies for acquiring information. Outline approaches for problem resolution. Establish criteria for evaluating the appropriateness of alternative solutions.)
5. Cognitive Strategies Internally organized skills whose function is to regulate and monitor the utilization of concepts and rules	1. *Discovery and guided discovery* (Involves more direct instruction than discovery, helping learners ascertain particular strategies through the application of questioning strategies.) 2. *Observation* (Observe a model demonstrating the use of the strategy by paired, cooperative learners, expert demonstration, and symbolic visual or textual representation by fictional character.) 3. *Guided participation* (Work with learners to determine characteristics of learning task, identify strategies to facilitate the task, and determine effective methods for employing the strategy.) 4. *Direct instruction* (Identify utility of the strategy. Provide overview of steps and their relation to strategy. Demonstrate the strategy. Illustrate examples and non-examples. Practice application of the strategy across gradually more difficult situations. Provide corrective feedback. Give explicit encouragement and guidance to transfer strategy to separate but appropriate context.)

TABLE 2 (continued)

Outcome	Grounded Events
6. **Attitudes** Choice behaviors that do not necessarily determine specific actions but do make certain classes of action more or less probable	1. *Demonstrate* desired behaviors representative of target attitude by a respected role. 2. *Practice* desired behavior associated with the desired attitude–another powerful tool in attitude formation and change (e.g., role playing and group discussions). 3. *Provide reinforcement* for the desired behavior (increases probability of the behavior recurring). 4. *Communicate persuasive messages* from highly credible sources. 5. *Create dissonance* by persuading learner to perform an important behavior that is counter-dissonant to the person's own attitude. Attitude change may result.
7. **Psychomotor Skills** Coordinated muscular movements that may be difficult to distinguish from intellectual skills	1. *Massed versus spaced practice* (Massed practice engages learners in one or a few intensive periods of practice. Spaced practice exposes learners to short practice sessions distributed over time.) 2. *Whole versus parts practice* (Whole practice is advisable if the task is simple, not meaningful in parts, made up of simultaneously performed parts, and has highly dependent parts, and if the learner is able to remember long sequences, has long attention spans, and is highly skilled.) 3. *Progressive parts practice* (If learners may have difficulties putting the parts together into a meaningful and well-executed whole.) 4. *Backwards chaining* (Where learners are exposed to and practice the last step and work their way to the first step.)

Note. From *Instructional Design* (2nd ed.) by P. L. Smith & T. J. Ragan (1999).

pressed by distance educators is that it takes far more time to grade assignments and manage communications during e-learning than it does in traditional settings. For both learners and educators, too many interactions may impede, rather than facilitate learning.

Educators often ask students to complete many assignments to demonstrate mastery of important skills and concepts. While their intentions are good, the

TABLE 3. Extended Design Evaluation Chart Used to Help Ensure Alignment of Instructional Strategy

Objective	Assessment Item	Instructional Strategy
1. Given a set of instructional objectives, generate conventional and/or performance-based cyber-tests that are congruent with targeted objectives (learner and context).	Major categories for descriptors to be included in the assessment rubric that will be used to evaluate criterion-referenced test (CRT) instruments. Descriptor specific to each category listed under Table 1.	Assignment #6 (Part II)–Generate assessment instrument. At the end of the instructional unit, ask learners to generate a conventional CRT, an assessment rubric, and/or a checklist. Assignment description to provide clues about the general form of the solution. Publish criteria for evaluating solutions.
	1. Goal-Centered Criteria 2. Learner-Centered Criteria 3. Context-Centered Criteria 4. Assessment-Centered Criteria	Learners to respond to the posted questions and post additional questions or comments about the information covered in this unit in the proper location on the course bulletin board system. Related questions should facilitate discussion of problem space.
2. Given a set of instructional situations, recognize when learner assessments are generated during systematic design process.	Learner assessments are created after _____ during the _____ phase of the systematic design process. 1. establishing instructional strategy, design 2. defining objectives, design 3. defining objectives, development 4. conducting goal analysis, analysis 5. selecting media, development	Read Dick, Carey, & Carey (2001), Chapter 7–"Developing Assessment Instruments." Chapter 7 addresses: 1. When learner assessments are addressed during systematic design process 2. Purposes of criterion-referenced testing 3. Methods for generating conventional criterion-referenced testing (CRT) instruments 4. Criteria for evaluating the quality of conventional CRT
3. Given a set of instructional situations, recall purposes of criterion-referenced testing (CRT).	Criterion-referenced tests can be used to measure students' entry-level behaviors. 1. true 2. false Criterion-referenced tests can be used to monitor students' progress toward specified learning objectives. 1. true 2. false	Read Unit 6.0 supplemental materials on Learner Assessment Methods. Supplemental reading addresses: 1. Alternative testing methods (compares and contrasts norm-referenced, conventional, criterion-referenced, and performance-based) 2. Purposes of performance-based CRT (portfolio and checklists)

TABLE 3 (continued)

Objective	Assessment Item	Instructional Strategy
4. Given a set of instructional situations, distinguish two forms of CRT.	The two basic forms of criterion-referenced tests are conventional and _____. 1. norm-referenced 2. fill-in-the-blank 3. product checklists 4. portfolio assessments 5. performance-based assessments	3. Key components of portfolio assessment methods 4. Key components of performance checklists 5. Methods for generating performance-based CRT (assessment rubrics and checklists) 6. Criteria for evaluating the quality of performance-based CRT Textbook and supplemental reading
5. Given a set of instructional situations, characterize key components of portfolio assessments.	Analytic performance assessments are based on 1. an overall impression of work samples. 2. different dimensions or components of work. 3. the conditions specified in the objectives. 4. varying performance levels or scales. 5. key learner characteristics and contextual factors. Portfolio assessments should include three key components, including 1. conventional tests, narrative, and objectives. 2. narrative, criteria, and assessment rubrics. 3. work samples, test instruments, and contracts. 4. narrative, work samples, and performance criteria. 5. work samples, analytic and holistic assessment rubrics.	
6. Given the results of a goal and subordinate skills analysis and a set of instructional objectives, generate and align assessment items by generating a design evaluation chart.	Product checklist items with two possible levels of performance: (a) yes, and (b) no, and an opportunity to comment. 1. Assessment method clearly defined and appropriate for context and objectives 2. Evaluation chart properly formatted 3. Specified skills consistent with those identified in goal and subordinate skills analyses 4. Objectives consistent with specified skills 5. Assessment items congruent with objectives	Assignment #6 (Part I)–Generate design evaluation chart that will be used to create assessment instruments. Description of assignment provides clues about the general form of the solution and criteria for evaluating alternative solutions. Learners to respond to the posted questions and post additional questions or comments about the information covered in this unit in the proper location on the course bulletin board system. Related questions should facilitate discussion of problem space.

consequences in terms of time management must be considered. In traditional classroom settings, students simply hand in assignments that the instructor stores until she or he is ready to grade. Review and evaluation take time, but written feedback may be brief because the instructor can supplement written comments with verbal explanations. During e-learning, the instructor must acknowledge receipt of assignments; save and store files; print out, review and assess each document; generate and distribute detailed feedback; and assure learners understand the feedback. That's at least five time-consuming tasks for every assignment. If you have 30 students and require them to complete 10 assignments, you may have to manage as many as 1,500 interactions per course. Considering the time and effort necessary to complete each interaction, it is easy to see why distance educators may feel overwhelmed during the delivery of an online course. The fact that written communication takes considerably more time to prepare and manage than oral communication further accentuates the importance of analyzing and balancing planned e-learning interactions.

In another article, I detail systematic methods for analyzing planned e-learning interactions (Hirumi, 2002b). In short, you may be able to determine if you have too many or too few interactions by examining the frequency and nature of planned learner-human and learner-nonhuman interactions (Table 4). In this article, I describe one specific tactic for balancing learner-instructor interactions that requires teamwork with a just evaluation of individual student contributions.

It takes considerably less time to manage and evaluate 6 group assignments, rather than 30 individual assignments–time you could spend on other tasks or providing more detailed and timely feedback. The challenge lies in designing group projects so that all participants learn and contribute equitably. Group work can be difficult enough when students meet regularly in class. At a distance, the basic challenges remain the same, but the methods used to overcome them may differ.

Successful group work requires effective planning and communications. Group members must contribute to the completion of assignments and a fair and accurate assessment must be made of each member's efforts. Specific tools and techniques are necessary to facilitate such vital group interactions online.

Job aids and published procedures for using e-mail, bulletin board systems and chat rooms can help ensure that distance learners have the skills necessary to telecommunicate. Training and information on (virtual) teamwork and group problem-solving skills may also help learners communicate with one another. To assess each person's contribution, you can ask learners to complete the assignment on their own before working with teammates to produce a final "group" assignment and ask group members to evaluate one another's work. The basic design of individual and group assignments in an online course illustrates how each of these techniques may be applied to optimize time spent online.

TABLE 4. Sample Analysis of Planned E-Learning Interactions

Interaction	Quantity	Quality	Design Decision
1. Learner-Content	21	1. One lesson overview page that provides description of and links to information about introduction, task, process, resources, evaluation, and conclusion. 2. Detailed descriptions of how to complete each of the 10 tasks associated with the process. 3. Links to 7 resources. 4. Two detailed evaluation rubrics. 5. Description of how to prepare and submit journal entry.	Interface very important to test prior to official course delivery
2. Learner-Instructor	8	1. Ask learner to post message. 2. Review and provide feedback on topic. 3. Review and provide feedback on problem statement. 4. Provide guidance on writing final report. 5. Provide guidance on preparing debriefing. 6. Assess and provide feedback on final report. 7. Assess and provide feedback on debriefing. 8. Review and provide feedback on journal entries.	Far too many interactions to manage (need to review and revise by grouping two or more interactions, grouping students, eliminating or further automating interactions)
3. Learner-Learner	5	1. Share short description of previously seen or written reports. 2. Share and discuss problem statements. 3. Share and discuss purpose statements. 4. Conduct peer reviews of reports. 5. Participate and share comments on debriefings.	May be too much (need review with particular attention during testing)
4. Learner-Other	2	1. Contact librarian. 2. Contact other professors.	Need to ensure librarian is prepared; need to ensure ready access to other professors
5. Learner-Environment	3	1. Go to library. 2. Acquire and read textbook. 3. Acquire and read journal articles.	Need to ensure ready access to library resource and textbook

Note. From "A framework for analyzing, designing and sequencing planned eLearning interactions" by A. Hirumi, 2002, Quarterly Review of Distance Education, 3(2), 141-160.

As soon as students register for a course, they are sent a welcome letter that provides directions for accessing the course and an online course orientation. During the orientation, students are asked to read through the course syllabus and complete a series of short activities to demonstrate their ability to use various telecommunications technologies. Students sign and submit a checklist to verify that they have completed the activities and are aware of important course policies and procedures.

The checklist also serves as a contract to help clarify roles and responsibilities and ensure learners have the required prerequisite skills and knowledge. If learners are not able to successfully complete the activities, they are required to either attend an optional face-to-face orientation held on campus during the first week of class, contact the instructor to determine an appropriate course of action, particularly if they cannot attend the face-to-face orientation, or they may be administratively dropped from the course.

During the first week, the goals are to ensure that learners (a) have a good understanding of course requirements and expectations, (b) can locate and interpret relevant policies and procedures, (c) are confident in their ability to use various tools and course features, and (d) can identify challenges associated with and discuss strategies for facilitating virtual teamwork. In addition to the online orientation materials, learners are asked to read several online articles on facilitating virtual teams and are reminded of the importance of interpersonal and virtual teamwork skills. If a problem should arise, group members are told to first attempt to work through issues on their own by identifying problems with process, not people, before contacting the instructor for help. Throughout the course, students are required to finish a series of both individual and group assignments to demonstrate achievement of course objectives.

For each instructional unit, students are directed to complete all required readings, a multiple-choice quiz covering key concepts contained in the readings, and an individual draft of the unit assignment. Although the unit assignment is actually a group project, each member is tasked with completing his or her own draft of the assignment to help ensure that everyone is learning to apply newly acquired skills and knowledge. Then group members are to share their experiences and work with team members to complete a group version of the assignment using e-mail, a private bulletin board forum, chat, and whatever form of communications the team prefers. The team posts one copy of their teamwork. If a team posts a draft of their work one week before the official due date, feedback is given based on published performance criteria from the instructor so that the team can revise their work before submitting it for a grade.

Each member is responsible for posting a copy of his or her individual draft, along with a short description of personal contributions, and for completing a teamwork evaluation for each member of the group. To minimize time spent online, individual drafts are evaluated based on a plus and minus system. Detailed review and feedback are reserved for the group version of the assignment. Teamwork evaluations consist of five measures: quality, timeliness, interpersonal skill, attitude, and quantity of contribution. Scores from each member of the team are averaged to derive a final score for each individual. The combination of individual and group assignments optimizes time spent online by limiting the number of assignments that must be evaluated and managed as an integral part of e-learning while also providing a fair assessment of each learner's work.

Create Feedback Templates

Feedback is vital to e-learning. At minimum, feedback is essential for closing message loops (Yacci, 2000; Northrup & Rasmussen, 2000), informing learners that communications are complete (Berge, 1999; Liaw & Huang, 2000; & Weller, 1988, as cited by Northrup, 2001). Feedback may also be used to (a) increase response rates or accuracy, (b) reinforce correct responses to prior stimuli, or (c) change erroneous responses (Kulhavy & Wager, 1993). During e-learning, telecommunications expand feedback options. Electronic mail, bulletin board systems, chat rooms, and audio and video conferencing may be used to provide immediate and delayed feedback and present learners with guidance, lesson sequence advisement, motivational messages, critical comparisons, and information about answer correctness and timeliness (Hoska, 1993). Without feedback, instruction may become "passing on content as it if were dogmatic truth, and the cycle of knowledge acquisition, critical evaluation, and knowledge validation that is important for the development of higher order thinking skills, is nonexistent" (Shale & Garrison, 1990, p. 29). From a learner's perspective, it is often the ability and commitment to provide immediate, detailed, and appropriate feedback that distinguishes a good online distance educator from a bad one.

Given the importance of feedback, how can we generate timely and detailed feedback in a relatively quick and efficient manner? You could limit enrollments or increase the number of people who provide the feedback, but, unfortunately, few of us are afforded such luxuries. You could also group students and ask them to complete group assignments, thereby reducing the total number of papers you have to review. No matter how many students you have or how they are arranged, templates may be created to optimize the time you spend generating feedback.

An effective feedback template consists of four primary components: (a) assessment criteria, (b) confirmatory feedback (c) corrective feedback, and (d) personalized messages. An example of the four components is depicted in Appendix 1.

Assessment criteria are derived from the design evaluation chart (see Table 1). To demonstrate achievement of the unit's terminal objective, students are to generate criterion-referenced assessment instruments. Figure 1 lists descriptors that characterize exemplary, proficient, and unsatisfactory criterion-refer-

FIGURE 1. Graphic Illustrating the Distinction Between a Horizontal and Vertical Prototype

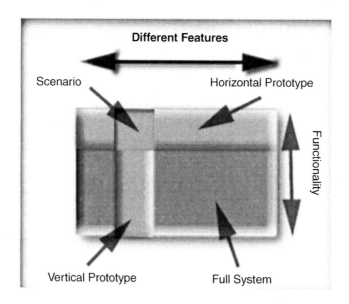

enced assessment instruments. The assessment criteria are published to help guide student effort, to assess student work, and to provide both confirmatory and corrective feedback.

Confirmatory feedback lets students know what they did correctly. Specific characteristics of student work listed in the assessment criteria may be highlighted in bold font to confirm exemplary performance. Additional comments provide further confirmatory feedback and highlight particular areas of proficient performance. Anecdotal reports from students indicate that starting with confirmatory feedback (letting students know the good aspects of their work) helps sustain their motivation.

Corrective feedback identifies areas that could or should be improved and provides students with insights on how to revise their work. Again, specific criteria may be highlighted in bold, but in this case, at the proficient and unsatisfactory levels to identify areas for improvement. In many cases, additional comments may be required to provide sufficient corrective feedback.

When confronted with a difficult assignment, students often make common errors. To generate detailed corrective feedback, I typically scan and select what appears to be the most inadequate work sample and grade it first. I assess the students' work and prepare a list of corrective comments. I then select what appears to be a model assignment and grade it to generate a list of positive confirmatory comments. I use both lists to create an initial feedback template that consists of the published assessment criteria and a list of confirmatory and corrective comments. The template saves me considerable time by allowing me to copy and paste appropriate comments rather than generating them each time I grade an assignment. As I grade other students' assignments, I add to the list of comments and continuously increase the comprehensiveness of the template.

Another way of using data on common errors is to identify apparent flaws in design and revise materials to prevent the recurrence of errors. Creating error-free environments, however, is not necessarily an effective e-learning strategy. Students can learn a lot from making and correcting mistakes, and the resulting cognitive dissonance may increase persistence and motivation. As a general rule of thumb, if 30% or more of the students make the same error on an assignment, I use the data to revise my instructional materials. If less than 30% make a particular error, I save my corrective feedback statements as an integral part of my feedback template for use in future classes.

When using feedback templates, it is important to demonstrate to students that you are evaluating each assignment individually. If students within a class receive virtually identical feedback, they may begin to think that you are rushing through their assignment and not spending adequate time properly assessing their work. Personalized messages integrated with the confirmatory and corrective feedback statements refer to unique aspects of student work and demonstrate that you are taking the time to properly read and review each assignment.

I inform students at the beginning of each course that I often use templates to assess assignments and provide feedback. I let them know that they may see similar comments if they compare feedback given to different students or teams of students on group projects. I tell them that feedback templates are the best way I've found to provide timely and detailed feedback and ask them to be certain to e-mail me if they have any questions concerning my feedback or feel that my comments are inappropriate. Student course satisfaction surveys suggest that the use of feedback templates is acceptable as long as students are informed of their use and receive detailed and appropriate feedback that includes personalized messages in a timely manner.

Establish Telecommunication Protocols

The use of interactive technologies does not ensure that meaningful interactions will occur. Telecommunications protocols that detail guidelines and performance requirements for posting bulletin board messages, chatting, and completing instructional units can increase the value of each experience and optimize time spent online.

Electronic Bulletin Board (BBS) Protocol

When properly integrated, an electronic bulletin board system (BBS) can facilitate e-learning, allowing students to generate and access a continuous dialog on specific topics when desired. In addition, students have time to read, think about, and construct thoughtful responses to posted comments and save entire discussions that can be organized over time. Simply providing access to a BBS, however, does not ensure that meaningful interactions will occur.

To optimize the value of a BBS, students must actively participate in and take responsibility for the discussions. They must have a clear purpose and the skills necessary to use the system. The discussions must also be well organized and easy to follow. Anything less and learners may perceive BBS postings as meaningless busy work. Students and instructors may become overwhelmed by a plethora of postings that take considerable time to read and interpret.

A protocol that I use to facilitate BBS discussions includes thought-provoking questions, organized discussion forums, published performance criteria, and student-generated summaries. Initially, I post a description of the BBS activity that describes the purpose and rationale for participating in the discussions. The description also includes guidelines and performance criteria for posting messages, a series of questions used to initiate the discussions, and an example of what I consider to be an appropriate posting that demonstrates critical thinking. The questions are organized by topic into various discussion forums so that students are participating in one to three discussions per unit.

During the first week of class, students are asked to review the BBS description and to rank the questions in priority order based on interest. I then randomly select students and assign one question based on prioritized list, to each student to facilitate discussion. The assignments are posted, along with due dates for each summary, and students are reminded to review the performance criteria before initiating the discussions (Table 5).

During each instructional unit, students are to post responses to the original questions and comment on other classmates' postings as they complete assigned readings and activities. Students are again reminded to extend discussions, rather then repeat what others may have already posted. I also scan the postings, offer comments, and ask students to elaborate on particularly insightful or interesting remarks. However, I do not read every posting. The student assigned to a particular question is responsible for facilitating and managing each discussion. I focus my attention on reviewing, assessing, and responding to the summary that is to be posted no later than one week after the class has finished a particular unit. In this manner, I can save time spent online, while still correcting misconceptions and addressing any key issues that students may have missed during each discussion.

TABLE 5. Performance Criteria Published for Facilitating Bulletin Board Communications

Distinguished (90-100 pts)	**Facilitates Thread (50 pts)** 1. Selects and actively facilitates one thread by posting multiple comments and soliciting additional comments 2. Researches topic and posts related findings 3. Summarizes one thread, identifying trends and patterns, noting discrepancies, and addressing original question 4. Posts summary in appropriate location and by specified due date **Actively Participates in Threads (50 pts)** 1. Actively participates (posts more than two comments) in at least one thread per unit other than his or her own 2. Posts comments that contain original idea or thought, building and elaborating on (rather than repeating) other messages 3. Posts all comments during appropriate times (when the majority of the class is working on the related unit and assignment)
Proficient (80-89 pts)	**Facilitates Thread** 1. Selects and facilitates one thread 2. Summarizes one thread addressing original question 3. Posts summary in appropriate location and by specified due date **Actively Participates in Threads** 1. Participates (posts 1 comment) in at least one thread per unit other than his or her own 2. Posts comments that demonstrate some original and critical thinking 3. Posts comments during appropriate times (when the majority of the class is working on the related unit and assignment)
Unsatisfactory (< 50 pts)	**Facilitates Thread** 1. Fails to select, facilitate, and/or summarize one thread 2. Posts summary in inappropriate location and/or past specified due date 3. Fails to participate in at least one thread per unit **Actively Participates in Threads** 1. Comments fail to demonstrate original or critical thinking 2. Comments not posted during appropriate times (when the majority of the class is working on the related unit and assignment)

Chat Protocol

Chat is an often used mode of communication for facilitating e-learning. The problem is that chat sessions with over six participants can be very difficult to follow. You also confine one of the benefits of e-learning if you require students to be at a certain location at a specific time and date. However, there are some advantages to chat. For instance, real-time, interactive dialog may be established between multiple users and conversations may be saved for review at a later time at relatively low cost.

Typically, I use chat for virtual "office hours." Students are informed that if they log on to chat at a specific time and date, they can chat with me about course assignments and activities. I do inform students that, if no one shows up during the initial 15 minutes of the specified start time, I will log off to avoid unnecessary time waiting to see if anyone will chime in. In my experience, three to five students participate in the optional sessions.

If instruction warrants a required chat with an entire class, I've found one useful method for facilitating the session. Similar to the BBS protocol (discussed above), I begin by posting a description of the scheduled chat sessions that includes a purpose statement, netiquette for communicating during each session (Table 6), and a list of planned events and expected outcomes.

At the beginning of the chat session, the entire class meets at the specified time and I quickly review the purpose, remind everyone to follow the posted netiquette, and assure that everyone understands the planned sequence of events and expected outcomes. Then I divide the class into small groups and ask each group to select a facilitator and a presenter. The small groups go into different chat rooms and the facilitator ensures that the group meets the targeted outcomes within the specified time frame. I go in and out of the various chat rooms to monitor progress and address any questions that may arise. After the small groups have finished chatting, everyone meets again in one room and I lead a discussion with the designated presenters to go over the results of each small group while others lurk and make note of any additional questions. Finally, at the end of the chat session, I do open the discussion to the entire group to address any lingering questions or comments. Depending on the purpose and relative importance of the chat session, I may ask each individual student to reflect on and post a short description of the insights gained during the

TABLE 6. Specific Netiquette for Facilitating Chat Sessions

1. When the instructor is present, key in on his or her comments and please follow his or her directions.

2. If you are directing your comment to a particular individual or responding to an individual's posting, type the person's name at the beginning of your message (e.g., John: I agree 100%, chat can be very useful if everyone adheres to specified protocols).

3. Keep messages fairly short. If you have a relatively long message, type ". . ." at the end of a few lines. That means that more is to come. Please do not post any new messages. If you see ". . ." typed at the end of message, hold your comments until the author has finished his or her comment.

4. Use abbreviations and emoticons whenever possible.

5. Do not worry about spelling. Everyone is typing as fast as he or she can during chat sessions.

Note. A link is provided to additional information and examples of emoticons.

chat session. Limiting most of the chat session to five to six active discussants, plus applying the prescribed netiquette and asking learners to reflect on the session can increase the educational value of the chat session while decreasing time spent online.

Unit/Lesson Protocol

Students can become confused and experience difficulties regulating their learning if requirements for completing a lesson or unit are located in different places. Online courses are typically made up of several components. Information and directions are often presented in a syllabus, course documents, assignments, calendar, e-mail, and bulletin board postings. As a result, students may not be able to readily discern the requirements necessary to successfully complete instruction or may be presented with contradictory directions or criteria if the instructor does not take the time to assure that everything is consistent. Instructors, in turn, may have to spend considerable time explaining procedures or remediating instruction that may have been missed or misunderstood. Revising and updating courses may also take considerable time when requirements are located in different areas and documents.

An effective tactic for organizing unit or lesson requirements is to generate an overview page. Appendix 2 illustrates the components of a sample unit overview page. Note that all assignments and activities necessary to complete the instructional unit are either presented or provided as a link from the overview page. In this manner, students can go to one location and get a good idea of what they must do to manage their time. Students also know that if they finish each of the events listed in the overview, they will have completed the unit.

Generate Prototypes to Formatively Evaluate Materials

Up to this point, I've discussed tactics for optimizing the time educators spend online facilitating the e-learning process. Each of the aforementioned tactics, however, may require you to spend additional time preparing e-learning materials prior to delivery. The final tactic focuses on decreasing the amount of time spent designing and developing materials.

Educators can spend a lot of time developing e-learning materials, only to find that significant revisions are necessary after initial implementation. Basic changes in navigation, structure, page layout, font styles, and instructional design may require considerable time and resources if they have to be applied to an entire course. Rather than developing all of the instructional units associated with a course, a more efficient method for creating e-learning materials is to first generate, test, and revise a horizontal and vertical prototype. The revised prototypes may then be used as a template for building the rest of your course.

A horizontal prototype presents students with a wide range of program features that are not yet fully functional. In contrast, vertical prototypes present students with relatively few program features that are fully functional (Figure 1).

For an online course, a horizontal prototype may consist of a course home page that provides access to most or all course features (e.g., syllabus, instructional units, calendar, assignments, telecommunications tools) but each feature may not be entirely operational. A vertical prototype may consist of one fully functional instructional unit, including objectives, content information, graphics, assignments, activities, tools, and assessments. With a vertical and horizontal prototype, you can test most key features of the user interface and the basic instructional design before going into full-scale production, preventing the need for costly revisions after significant portions of the e-learning program have been programmed. The vertical prototype may then be used as a template for all other instructional units as well as a basis for establishing standards for navigation, font size, font style, the use of headings, placement, and size of graphics.

WHAT'S THE PAY OFF?

The tactics discussed in this article require time and expertise–vital resources that may be spent on other important tasks. It takes time and expertise to analyze an instructional situation; generate, cluster, and sequence objectives; prepare and design evaluation charts; and align objectives, assessments, and instructional events. It takes time and expertise to analyze and balance interactions, create feedback templates, establish telecommunications protocols, and generate and test horizontal and vertical prototypes.

To further complicate matters, it may be more difficult to convince others to adopt the tactics posited in this article than it is to apply them. The products (e.g., design documents, feedback templates, unit overview pages, telecommunications protocols) are not flashy and may not attract relevant stakeholders. The compulsion for results may preclude design. Educators are being pressed to post courses and provide access, rather than ensure quality. A focus on tangible products without sufficient planning, however, may lead to a false sense of economy. The effects of poorly designed instruction may not be felt until later when learners are asked to build on skills and concepts that they may not have mastered. If courses are poorly designed, dissatisfied learners may also drop out and warn others to avoid the program. Unfortunately, high-quality online courses that optimize the time both students and instructors spend online may not be sufficient to convince key decision makers to allocate the necessary resources; not because quality students and instructors are unimportant, but because the perceived gains in quality, learning, and satisfaction are not believed to be worth the investment.

To garner resources, keep in mind that the tactics yield transferable skills and products when estimating the return on investment. The tactics are worth the time and effort because the resulting skills and materials may be used more than once with as many learners as possible. Often, the person who authors a course must teach it because she or he is the only one that knows how to address gaps or flaws in design. The tactics posited in this paper help ensure that all of the elements necessary to facilitate e-learning are aligned and contained in the materials. This does not mean that an instructor is not necessary. Rather, instructors with the proper qualifications and experiences should be able to teach the course with relatively little investment prior to or during course delivery. In addition, the instructor who originally developed the online course may also use the skills and materials to improve the quality of his or her other courses. The transferability of skills, knowledge, and products to enhance both online and face-to-face courses has been reported as one of the key benefits derived from distance education training and the systematic design of e-learning materials (Hirumi, Arneson, & Chandler, 2001).

To ensure the long-term success of e-learning programs, we must find methods for optimizing the amount of time spent online. To reduce time spent directing and clarifying the e-learning process, you can align instructional objectives, assessment, and events; prepare feedback templates, and establish telecommunication protocols. To optimize time spent developing e-learning materials, you can begin by designing, developing, testing, and revising one instructional unit and use vertical and horizontal prototypes as templates to facilitate the development of remaining units. One question still remains: given time and resources to generate high-quality materials, will it still take more time to facilitate e-learning than traditional classroom instruction?

Some argue that e-learning takes more time to facilitate than traditional face-to-face instruction because, fundamentally, it takes more time to generate and transmit written rather than oral communications. Certainly, reading and writing take more time than speaking and listening. However, this does not mean that e-learning materials cannot be designed to optimize time spent online. The perceived need for additional resources may simply mean that e-learning, as a field, is still in its infancy. We are just beginning to learn how to redesign teacher-directed methods and materials, transform the teaching and learning process, and produce quality e-learning materials in a cost-effective manner. Educators are urged to continue seeking and testing new methods for optimizing the use of emerging telecommunications technologies. If we don't, others more interested in granting degrees than ensuring quality may dominate the e-learning market and like other distance education programs, the value of degrees and course credit earned online may remain suspect.

REFERENCES

Berge, Z. L. (1999). Interaction in post-secondary Web-based learning. *Educational Technology, 39*(1), 5-11.

Berge, Z. L. (2002). Active, interactive and reflective e-learning. *Quarterly Review of Distance Education, 3*(2), 181-190.

Dick, W., Carey, L., & Carey, J. O. (2001). *The systematic design of instruction* (5th ed.). New York: Addison-Wesley.

Gagne, R. M. (1977). *The Conditions of Learning* (3rd ed.). New York: Holt, Rinehart, & Winston.

Gilbert, L., & Moore, D. R. (1998). Building interactivity into Web courses: Tools for social and instructional interactions. *Educational Technology, 38*(3), 29-35.

Hannafin, M. J., Hannafin, K. M., Land, S. M., & Oliver, K. (1997). Grounded practice and the design of learning systems. *Educational Technology Research and Development, 45*(3), 101-117.

Hirumi, A. (2002a). Designing and sequencing eLearning interactions: A grounded approach. *International Journal on E-Learning, 1*(1), 19-27.

Hirumi, A. (2002b). A framework for analyzing, designing and sequencing planned eLearning interactions. *Quarterly Review of Distance Education, 3*(2), 141-160.

Hirumi, A., Arneson, W., & Chandler, K. (2001). *Training faculty on the systematic design of e-learning.* Concurrent session presented at the annual Texas Distance Learning Association Conference, Houston, TX.

Hoska, D. M. (1993). Motivating learners through CBI feedback: Developing a positive learner perspective. In J. V. Dempsey & G. C. Sales (Eds.), *Interactive instruction and feedback* (pp. 105-32). Englewood Cliffs, NJ: Educational Technology.

Jonassen, D. H., Tessmer, M., & Hannum, W. H. (1999). *Task analysis methods for instructional design.* Mahwah, NJ: Lawrence Erlbaum.

Kulhavy, R. W., & Wager, W. (1993). Feedback in programmed instruction: Historical context and implications for practice. In J. V. Dempsey & G. C. Sales (Eds.), *Interactive instruction and feedback* (pp. 2-20). Englewood Cliffs, NJ: Educational Technology.

Liaw, S., & Huang, H. (2000). Enhancing interactivity in Web-based instruction: A review of the literature. *Educational Technology, 40*(3), 41-45.

Northrup, P. (2001). A framework for designing interactivity in Web-based instruction. *Educational Technology, 41*(2), 31-39.

Northrup, P. T., & Rasmussen, K. L. (2000, February). *Designing a Web-based program: Theory to design.* Paper presented at the annual conference of the Association for Educational Communications and Technology, Long Beach, CA.

Shale, D., & Garrison, D. R. (1990). Education and communication. In D. R. Garrison & D. Shale (Eds.), *Education at a distance* (pp. 23-39). Malabar, FL: Robert E. Krieger.

Smith, P. L., & Ragan, T. J. (1999). *Instructional design* (2nd ed.). Upper Saddle River, NJ: Prentice-Hall.

Weller, H. G. (1988). Interactivity in microcomputer-based instruction: Its essential components and how it can be enhanced. *Journal of Educational Technology Systems, 28*(2), 23-27.

Yacci, M. (2000). Interactivity demystified: A structural definition for distance education and intelligent computer-based instruction. *Educational Technology, 40*(4), 5-16.

APPENDIX 1
Feedback Template for Assignment on Generating a Criterion-Referenced Test

INST5333: Systematic Design of Instruction **A6: Assessment and Feedback**	
Name(s):	**Date: 10/15/01**
Performance Criteria for Learner Assessment Items	**(/100pts)**
Exemplary (90-100pts)	**Goal-Centered Criteria** • Match behavior, including the action and concepts prescribed in objectives • Meet conditions specified in the objectives **Learner-Centered Criteria** • Tailored to learners in terms of vocabulary, language levels, developmental levels, motivational and interest levels, experiences, backgrounds, and special needs • Free of gender, ethnic, or cultural biases **Context-Centered Criteria** • Realistic or authentic to actual performance setting as possible • Feasible and suited to resources available in learning setting **Assessment-Centered Criteria** • Applies correct grammar, spelling, and punctuation • Stem clearly formulates problem (worded so that learner can easily determine what problem or question is being asked before reading possible answers) • Stem contains task and most information, keeping answers/ options short • Stem includes only required information and written in a clear, positive manner • Foils include only one correct, defensible, best answer • Foils are plausible and do not contain unintentional clues to correct answer (e.g., length, all, never, a, an)

Comments

Overall, your design evaluation chart and assessment instrument demonstrate XXX performance as noted above. Your assessment items are clearly aligned to your analysis and objectives and are congruent with learners and context–very well done.

I do have XX comments that I would like you to consider:

- My greatest concern lies in your first row. There appears to be a discrepancy in the skills identified in column one of your design evaluation chart and (a) the skills and knowledge identified in your subordinate skills analysis; and (b) the behaviors stated in objective 3.0 and the assessment items listed in row one, column three. I do not see self-assessed prior knowledge and materials in your subordinate skills analysis. Furthermore, your objective asks learners to enter content (not self assess).

- Questions X is unclear. The assessment-centered criteria for generating learner assessments (Activity A) specifies that stems should clearly formulate problem (worded so that learner can easily determine what problem or question is being asked before reading possible answers). I had to read your question over several times before I could figure out what you were asking.

- Question X appears to have two correct answers (access and selection). The assessment-centered criteria for generating learner assessments (Activity A) specifies that the stem include only one correct or clearly best answer.

- The stem in question X is written in negative manner (". . . is *not* one . . ."). The assessment-centered criteria for generating learner assessments (Activity A) suggest that stems be written in positive manner. Although it is not totally inappropriate to make both stem and options negative in the same item and also bad practice to write either stem or options in negative fashion for children. Again, question 1 is not "incorrect." I just want to encourage you to write questions and answers in a positive manner.

- Although I do believe that experts can name the authors of key concepts and theories (e.g., question 2), I am not particularly a fan of such assessment items (I believe Einstein wrote, "I never memorize anything I can look up." Although the same may be said for questions 1 and 3, I like them better because they are more conceptual in nature).

- The stem and the correct answer for question 2 include the word "behavior." I think this may provide learners with an unintentional clue to the correct answer. Note: The performance criteria for Activity A specifies that "foils are plausible and do not contain any unintentional clues to correct answer."

I hope you find my comments useful. Be sure to let me know if you have any questions or comments.

2c

APPENDIX 2

Sample Unit Overview Page that Includes All Recommended Instructional Events

Course Logo	INST5333: Systematic Design of Technology-Based Instruction **Unit 7.0–Learner Assessment Methods**

Objectives | Resources | Events | References

Unit Overview

Criterion-referenced tests (CRT) are designed to measure student achievement of an explicit set of learning objectives. Conventional tests include multiple-choice, true-false, fill-in-the-blank, matching, and short answer items. Such tests have become pervasive because they could be mass-produced, administered, and scored with relative objectivity. However, over the past decade, there has been a movement toward the increased use of performance assessments. To complete this unit, you are to create a design evaluation chart and an assessment instrument for your unit of instruction. You may choose to develop a conventional criterion-referenced test, a performance checklist, or a portfolio assessment rubric. Unit 7 should take you approximately 15 hours to complete.

[top]

Unit Objectives

Terminal Objective–Given a set of instructional objectives, develop conventional criterion-referenced tests, performance checklists or portfolio assessment rubrics that are congruent with specified learning objectives and learner characteristics for your unit of instruction.

Enabling Objectives–Given an instructional situation, you should be able to:

• identify characteristics of criterion-referenced test and portfolio assessments;

• compare and contrast traditional CRTs (e.g., multiple-choice, true-false, matching, and short answer tests), performance checklists, and portfolio assessment methods; and

• discuss performance criteria associated with generating learner assessment instruments.

[top]

Required Resources

• Unit 7.0–Learner Assessment Methods (online)

• Dick, W., Carey, L., & Carey, J. O. (2000). The systematic design of instruction: Chapter 7–Developing assessment instruments (pp. 140-174). New York: Addison-Wesley.

• List of performance objectives for your instructional unit

• Your learner analysis report

[top]

Recommended Instructional Events

1. Review Dick & Carey (1996), Chapter 7–Developing Assessment Instruments
2. Go through Unit 7.0–Learner Assessment Methods (online)
3. Complete Unit 7.0 Quiz (required)
4. Complete Assignment #7
5. Post any questions or comments you may have about Unit 7.0 in the proper location on the course Bulletin Board.

[top]

References

- Arter, J. A., & Spandel, V. (1992). *Using portfolios of student work in instruction and assessment. Educational measurement: Issues and practices*. OR: Northwest Regional Educational Laboratory.

- Berk, R. A. (Ed.). (1986). *Performance assessment: Methods and applications.* Baltimore, MD: Johns Hopkins University Press.

- Herman, J. L., Aschbacher, P. R., & Winters, L. (1992). *A practical guide to alternative assessment.* VA: Association for Supervision and Curriculum Development.

[top]

Determining If Distance Education Is the *Right* Choice:
Applied Strategic Thinking in Education

SUMMARY. Making decisions about which technologies, if any, are appropriate for your classroom or educational institution has never been easy. These difficult decisions are, however, increasing in their complexity as new technologies continually enter the marketplace, expectations of parents and students rise for more technology in the classroom, budget constraints require institutions to do more with less, and the benefits of distance education place mounting pressures on educators to provide resources beyond the boundaries of the traditional classroom. So how do you as an educational leader make the challenging decisions related to distance education and other technologies in your school? This article provides a framework for results-focused decision making that can help you make complicated choices in even the most challenging of circumstances. *[Article copies available for a fee from The Haworth Document Delivery Service: 1-800-HAWORTH. E-mail address: <docdelivery@haworthpress.com> Website: <http://www.HaworthPress.com> © 2003 by The Haworth Press, Inc. All rights reserved.]*

RYAN WATKINS is Assistant Professor, Department of Educational Leadership, Educational Technology Leadership Program, The George Washington University, Washington, DC 20052 (E-mail: rwatkins@gwu.edu).

[Haworth co-indexing entry note]: "Determining If Distance Education Is the *Right* Choice: Applied Strategic Thinking in Education." Watkins, Ryan. Co-published simultaneously in *Computers in the Schools* (The Haworth Press, Inc.) Vol. 20, No. 3, 2003, pp. 103-120; and: *Distance Education: What Works Well* (ed: Michael Corry, and Chih-Hsiung Tu) The Haworth Press, Inc., 2003, pp. 103-120. Single or multiple copies of this article are available for a fee from The Haworth Document Delivery Service [1-800-HAWORTH, 9:00 a.m. - 5:00 p.m. (EST). E-mail address: docdelivery@haworthpress.com].

KEYWORDS. Educational decision making, distance education, educational technology, system planning, strategic planning

In recent years the shifting and evolving responsibilities of leaders in education has created the requirement for dynamic models of decision making. For decades, educational institutions have benefited from the application of the conventional models for decision making that were derived from nearly a century of industrial growth. And while these models were quite useful in the rather stable educational environment that dominated most of the twentieth century, education has been rapidly changing with the development of information technologies and an expanding globalization (of all sectors, including both private and public). Leaders of today's institutions are increasingly being held accountable for supporting the growth of dynamic learners: learners that increasingly bring rapidly changing requirements to the *learning environment.*

Meeting these demands will require not only a new perspective on education, but also a new set of tools for institutional leaders. Building on the decision analysis techniques and visionary leadership tools, this article provides a pragmatic offering that can assist decision makers at all levels of an institution in making and justifying tough decisions related to education. Though the strategic thinking tools described are applicable to all of the difficult decisions educators are being asked to make, the primary context for the discussion will focus on the answer to one, not so simple question: *Is distance education "right" for me and/or my institution?*[1]

Additionally, the framework I described for systemically determining if distance education is the *correct* solution for you and/or your institution will also provide essential information for determining which (if any) intervention or technology is likely to accomplish the necessary results for you and/or your institution to be successful now and in the future. You can further use the decision-making framework to align daily activity and resource decisions with other critical decisions for the long-term health of the institution.

DISTANCE EDUCATION IS ONLY ONE OPTION

When making challenging decisions, if you begin with a predetermined solution (e.g., distance education, outsourcing, computer technologies, standardized tests, etc.), you are likely risking the long-term health of your institution. And while we often enter decision-making processes aware of the many pressures from different interest groups and with our own ideas as to what solution(s) may be appropriate, we do not want to presume that this limited perspective is going to accomplish the necessary results for institutional success now and in the future. Without a formal identification of the need (i.e., a gap in results), solutions are left to searching for problems for which they may be appropriate, and this is backward decision making.

Instead, we want to begin by examining what results are required for the long-term success of the institution, identify gaps between where we are and where we should be, and then (and only then) determine which solutions may be feasible for accomplishing the required results. And this is achieved through integrated strategic planning and needs assessment within a performance accomplishment system (Watkins & Leigh, 2001; Kaufman, Oakley-Brown, Watkins, & Leigh, 2003).

Since we are not starting with distance education as the pre-selected solution, this is likely not the path toward answering the question above (i.e., is distance education right for me and/or my institution) that you may have expected. Additionally, this article is not written to sell you on the benefits of *distance education* or any other tool that educational institutions may use to accomplish desired results. *Distance education*, as we will view it, is just one of many alternatives that may be *right* for ensuring individual and institutional success. Therefore, we will focus our attention on first ensuring that we *really know* the results that we want to (and must) achieve and how those are aligned with the requirements of the institution and the social system, before we examine the tools and techniques for selecting appropriate useful interventions (like distance education). This assessment-first approach is a hallmark of performance-based decision making (Watkins & Leigh, 2001).

A framework for integrated strategic planning and needs assessment can assist institutional leaders in setting strategic direction and accomplishing useful results (see Kaufman, 1998, 2000). The framework provides for the development and communication of a clear direction for educational institutions. By focusing on results and consequences, the planning and assessment approach to strategic thinking leads institutions away from decision making based on fads, trends, or knee-jerk reaction and toward a holistic approach of balancing the emerging results requirements of learners, institutions, and society with an agile and strategic decision-making structure. And distance education is thereby offered as one valuable alternative for institutional leaders to consider when determining how useful results will be achieved by and for their institution.

PREPARING FOR CHANGE

In his book *Adaptive Enterprises* (1999, p. 16), Stephan Haeckel, of IBM's Advance Business Institute, suggests that in "environments of discontinuous change, thinking outside the box is not sufficient: It is also necessary to think about changing the box." *Changing the box* of education, however, requires more of institutional leaders than merely choosing the correct technology or implementing a unique delivery model. Changing the box, and subsequently meeting the demands of the changing environment, requires that leaders guide institutions toward demonstrated added-value for learners and clients with varying perspectives and criteria for success (see Kaufman, Oakley-Brown, Watkins, & Leigh, 2003).

Achieving success in education, now and in the future, will not be the result of any singular software program, innovation, academic model, or policy change. Adding value for learners and clients will likely be achieved through a variety of interventions aligned with the unique requirements of the educational system. Throughout education, this may lead to a number of diverse yet successful institutional structures, dissimilar institutional objectives, assorted delivery models, and an array of other differences as educators identify distinct methods for adding value. And most of these changes required for success lie beyond the boundaries of our current approaches to education.

It has been evident in the evolution of information technologies that even the most capable leaders cannot systematically and accurately predict change, let alone predict changes at the rapid pace that would be demanded by today's institutions. So how can we as leaders of education and training find success in the future without making meaningless predictions? Peter Drucker (1993), in his book *Post-Capitalist Society*, urges that if we are unable to accurately predict the future, then we should be concerned with creating the future. This proactive mindset is a brand feature of institutions that find success in emerging paradigms.

Proactively changing our institutions requires that we move forward into the new realities without quite knowing all the facts. This is not to suggest that leaders blindly storm off with any fad that may be disguised as an emerging paradigm; rather, successful leaders should structure their institutions in such a way that as the boundaries and ground rules shift, so does the institution. Institutions are thus adaptive and agile structures that can respond to change. The systemic thinking and planning model presented in this article is a guide for how leaders in education can approach *distance education* as one possible means for assisting the institution in achieving the dynamic characteristics necessary for demonstrating added value and finding continued success amid changing realities.

ESSENTIAL RELATIONSHIPS

Proactive systemic decision making is built on three foundational relationships. The first is the connection of system and systems thinking, the second is the affiliation of ends and means, and the third is the confusion of needs and wants. Each of these relationships, as the basis for the performance-based decision-making process, is essential for success.

System and Systems Thinking

The first relationship that should be explored as an essential basis for decision making is that of *system* and *systems* thinking. Though often used synonymously in the professional literature, the two approaches to thinking, planning, and assessing actually represent interrelated but distinct paradigms for institutional leaders who apply them. In practice, exemplary decision making regarding the appropriateness of *distance education*, or other initiatives, relies on both system and systems approaches that are applied in a systematic and systemic fashion.

Initially, any discussion of the essential relationships of *system* and *systems* approaches may seem like an unnecessary confusion of terms or semantic quibbling. But then when systemic and systematic processes to each approach are discussed, are we really going too far? I don't believe so. It is through the integration of both *system* and *systems* thinking that decision makers can plan for and assess *distance education* options with a complete understanding of both the entire array of success measures (system-wide perceptions) as well as the dynamic relationships among the interdependent systems (Kaufman, Watkins, & Leigh, 2001; Kaufman & Watkins, 2000). In application, when planning becomes implementation, the essential characteristics of systemic and systematic are critical to success.

In *Useful Educational Results* (2001, p. 16), Kaufman et al. offer the following definitions:

> *A system approach* begins with the sum total of parts working independently and together to achieve a useful set of results at the societal level, adding value for all internal and external partners such as our institution, employees, state, and the shared society. We best think of it as the large whole as represented as in Figure 1.

FIGURE 1. A System Approach

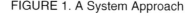

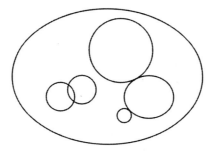

A systems approach begins with the *parts* of a system (i.e., subsystems) that make up the system, such as the training units, curriculum departments, as well as administrative and technology subsystems. The relationship among parts can be developed, analyzed, and/or evaluated, as represented as in Figure 2.

It should be noted here that a *system* is made up of contributing *systems* or subsystems. If we start at the subsystems level with a systems approach, we will start with only one part (or multiple individual parts) of the overall system (or supersystem) while ignoring the whole system. Thus, a systems approach really focuses solely on one or more subsystems. Though often well intentioned, it is usually a superficial focus on the parts rather than the whole. We commonly find examples of systems approaches in the practice of medicine, where a team of specialized physicians may each separately treat ailments related to the heart, lungs, digestion, and other subsystems, leaving the well-being of the whole system (i.e., your overall health) unattended. When making decisions with a *systems* approach, we can only *assume* that the payoffs and consequences will add up to something useful for the *system*, and that is usually a very big assumption.

In order to accomplish the many results that are essential for the varied perspectives on success of any educational institution, the system approach should serve as the basis for decision making since it alone ensures that all perspectives are included (e.g., parents, students, instructors, legislators, social service organizations, etc.). A systems approach, though effective in identifying and defining the success measures of a limited number of perspectives related to individual subsystems, does not provide decision makers with this

FIGURE 2. A Systems Approach

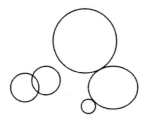

wide lens for viewing the array of criteria that must be met for an institution to be considered successful from diverse perspectives.

Having a system approach, in application, means that decision makers view success within the terms of their own institution (e.g., long-term profits, graduated students, and such) as well as their position (e.g., courses designed, CD-Roms developed, and such). But success from a system approach also includes the success criteria defined by external clients and partners (including, for example, learners, future employers, parents, community partners, resource suppliers, and other external partners). So, in applying a system approach to decision making, we start by removing the boundaries that have been the benchmarks for decision makers in the past.

Ends and Means

Beyond the relationship of system and systems approaches, another relationship that should be considered prior to making critical decisions regarding the application of *distance education* solutions is that of *ends* and *means*. Though the terms *ends* and *means* are common in our everyday language, we rarely take the time for close consideration of their relationship when making decisions. Ordinarily, we select our means with good faith that the desired ends will be the result of our labor. The more effort we put into an initiative, the more likely favored accomplishments are to be attained. But is this really true?

Our experiences have often reinforced the fact that decisions are commonly made in most of today's institutions without a clear and measurable end in mind (i.e., results or accomplishments). Rarely are institutional leaders able to define and communicate in measurable terms the ends, results, or accomplishments that they want to achieve through their institutions. Now this isn't to say that these leaders have not been quite successful in the past, because many of them have. In the past, when success could be defined by graduation rates and test scores alone, institutional leaders often did know the educational program, software upgrade, or process improvement tactic that would lead to success.

However, the options have grown, the competition for financial resources has increased, and the ability for leaders instinctively to know what solutions will be able to accomplish the necessary goals for the institution is challenged almost daily. As a result, successful decision makers today have learned to rely on performance data and clear operational definitions of success when making difficult decisions. This perspective is, however, most useful when the focus is on the results (i.e., ends) to be accomplished rather than on the implementation of the processes (i.e., means).

Needs and Wants

The final essential relationship we will discuss is that of *needs* and *wants*. Like the previously described relationships, this, too, is a relationship that is often muddled by the daily use of the terms as if they were synonyms. And while their mixed uses may be grammatically correct, it is the confusion of the terms that leads institutional leaders away from a result-focused process for decision making. In actuality, overuse of the term *need* may even be a little more devious than the confusion surrounding the earlier relationships.

For decades marketing companies have insisted on changing the vernacular of consumers in order to define *needs* as all the products that they want us to purchase. Marketing companies have been so successful in these efforts that it is now common for most children and adults to truly believe that they *"need"* the latest products on the market. Politicians even use the word *need* to add an exclamation when they want voters to support the activities they have in mind. We even find examples of a misperception in needs throughout our institutions everyday. For example, how often have you heard colleagues describe a product they "need" in order to do their job? The newest software? A new computer? Training on the latest management technique? Courses on gun safety in our schools? The list of preselected solutions goes on and on. But how does this aid the decision maker when trying to determine which of these activities is really going to accomplish the required results.

Unfortunately, often perceived solutions (e.g., software, computers, training, distance education, school vouchers, etc.) are not the singular solutions to the complex challenges of today's educational institutions. Yet, when reading the professional literature or attending a professional conference, you are commonly bombarded with people selling you on the notion that you "need" their solution to fix whatever challenges you may be facing in your institution.

While these products that we supposedly "need" may be appropriate tools or techniques for accomplishing some of our goals. Most often there are many alternatives that we no longer consider once the *need* has been defined by the marketing firm, the politician, sales person, or even the decision maker who is more concerned about the means than the ends. In order to keep all viable options open until the alternatives have been weighed, the relationship of *needs* and *wants* should be clarified.

In decision making, *needs* are best defined in relation to results. We can, therefore, define *needs* as gaps between the current results being achieved and those results that must be achieved for success (see Watkins, Leigh, Platt, & Kaufman, 1998). This discrepancy definition of needs, we suggest, is the basis for effective strategic planning, needs assessment, and decision making.

When *needs* are defined in terms of gaps in results, and not desired resources or activities, decision makers are better able to clearly define what results must be accomplished and select appropriate interventions (e.g., *distance education*) without the biases of a single-solution mind-set. Thus, the discrepancy definition of needs changes the language that decision makers use when identifying and addressing issues within their institutions. Effective decision makers no longer start a conversation with "we need to buy XYZ software" or "our staff needs more training on XYZ." Rather than prematurely selecting a solution in search of a problem, decision makers maintain a focus on the gap between current and required results with statements like, "our students are scoring 10 points below the set objective for our school on the state writing exam; what alternatives are available to help us improve?" or "employees are not able to process client orders using the software system; how can this be corrected?"

Necessity is not an established fact, but an interpretation.

–Friedrich Nietzsche
(as cited in BrainyMedia.com, 2002)

As a basis for the tools and techniques that will follow, we want to develop a framework for effective decision making. This framework will provide the foundational constructs for the processes that will hopefully quickly become intrinsic to your decision making. The framework, we suggest, is grounded in a system focus that takes into consideration the multiple perspectives of success, including that of the community (i.e., society). Further, it retains a results (i.e., performance) focus throughout, linking choices among alternative processes and resources to the accomplishment of useful results.

It is not, however, intended for this framework to provide a detailed and complex process for making decisions. System decision making is not an invariable set of procedures. It is a flexible and dynamic heuristic that is effective in selecting the appropriate course of action. Ideally, the framework will be illustrated in such a way that it becomes a basic construct that is not memorized, but rather one that you find to elaborate on the common-sense approaches to decision making that you have already developed.

A PERFORMANCE ACCOMPLISHMENT SYSTEM

A generalized performance accomplishment system offers a basic framework that is useful when considering decisions at the individual or institutional level. With a constant focus on accomplishing useful results, a performance accomplishment system can provide decision makers with a map for navigating through the necessary logic in making rational decisions that can be justified and are linked to performance.

While a variety of performance accomplishment systems share characteristics, the system illustrated in Figure 3 can serve as a basis for decisions related to *distance education* or most any alternative being considered at your institution. Initially developed as a tool for institutional performance improvement, the systematic approach profiled in the performance system delineates six essential steps in making decisions (and one step related to implementation and continuous improvement).[2] This framework provides the required comprehensive model for making effective choices, without the distraction of more complex systems designed for specific applications.

FIGURE 3. A Performance Accomplishment System

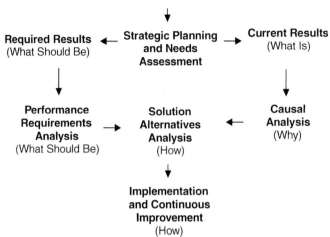

With a foundation in systematic planning and assessment, the performance accomplishment framework provides decision makers with the basic elements necessary for making (and justifying) difficult decisions. And while it could be viewed as a set of linear steps to be taken in selecting appropriate interventions (or solutions), it may be most useful when forgotten (or more accurately, developed as an intrinsic heuristic to guide decision making).

Decision making is not an invariable process. With each decision we make, whether personal or professional, we instinctively process information in varying sequences depending on the situation. Sometimes we first refer back to similar decisions in the past in order to determine the effectiveness of our previous decision-making processes. Other times we may react quickly to the new decision; only later do we examine how the situation was related to previous decisions. Most of us do, however, have a basic framework we commonly use to represent the effective decision-making processes we have identified from past experiences. But many times we are not conscious of the process, nor have we ever committed it to paper.

The general performance accomplishment system can provide a valuable decision-making heuristic for each of us. Even upon initial examination, the performance system likely seems logical and rather easy to apply. And it is. That is why my goal is not that readers will memorize the elements or the illustrations, but rather that the framework will become an intrinsic framework that you will refer to instinctively when presented with a challenging decision.

Strategic Planning and Needs Assessment

Strategic planning (and thinking) is the basis for long-term and short-term decision making. By identifying measurable objectives for the future, the strategic plan of an institution or individual should provide the guiding direction for all decisions made within the institution. Now this is probably more idealistic than what most of our experiences have been with strategic planning in the past, where strategic plans are written by institutional executives and then left on the shelf to gather dust until the next generation of leadership comes along to write a plan of their own.

So, how do strategic plans become *living documents* and thus guides for decision making? This is accomplished through integrated needs assessment. The needs assessment process is one that identifies and prioritizes gaps between current and required results in relation to the strategic plan. Using this definition, then, strategic planning and needs assessment are interrelated processes and they must coexist in order for either to add value. This companionship of these two processes provides the basis for either process leading to useful results, and together they will provide the foundation for effective decision making with regards to *distance education*.

Strategic planning and needs assessment processes are interdependent by their very nature (though commonly separated within most institutions). Useful strategic planning is dependent upon data related to current results being achieved by the institution, as well as data regarding the gaps between those current results and the current objectives required for success. And these data are best supplied through a results-focused needs assessment. The needs assessment, however, relies on the strategic plan as well. Since the needs assessment identifies gaps between current and desired (i.e., required) results, the process is dependent upon the strategic plan for definition of the latter. Without the strategic plan, there would be no gap, and without the needs assessment, the strategic planning process would be without data for setting useful objectives. So the integration of the two processes is critical to the success of either.

Required Results

Required results define for an institution, and the individuals that make up the institution, the objectives to be accomplished in achieving success for internal as well as external partners and clients. And while conventional strategic planning initiatives may have set out to define in measurable terms the long-term and short-term ambitions of the institution, missing from conventional approaches is the system perspective. The system perspective, as discussed previously, includes the views on success held by representative participants in the system, and not solely the institution itself nor individual groups within the system. In application, the incorporation of multiple perspectives on success requires more robust and inclusive visions, missions, and objectives than most institutions today currently have as their guide for decision making (Kaufman, Stith, Triner, & Watkins, 1998).

The defining of required results to be accomplished by, and for, educational institutions is an essential process in making decisions related to the appropriateness of distance education for an institution. Without clear linkage and alignment with the institution's goals and objectives, decisions regarding the implementation of distance education solutions may lead the institution away from identified goals and objectives. To ensure the necessary linkage and alignment, the application of a system-focused strategic planning model is suggested.

There are three levels of goals and objectives that are foundation to a system perspective. The first level defines results that are required for the long-term success of the society; Kaufman et al. (2001, 2003) refer to planning at this level as *mega planning*, where the primary client and beneficiary of the goals and objectives is the society in which the institution exists. When planning at the *mega* level, the institution has the opportunity to define its contribution (and thereby worth) within the context of the community.[3] This is the essential starting place for decision making that is going to lead to long-term success of the institution.

The second level of goals and objectives includes a focus on the institution. Kaufman et al. (2001, 2003) describes this level of planning as *macro planning*, with the primary client and beneficiary being the institution itself. Here the institution aligns its mission with the required results of the external community.[4] Based on this mission, the institution can then identify the goals and objectives for the individuals and departments within the institution. Planning at this level is *micro planning*, with the primary client and beneficiary being the individuals and small groups within the institution.[5] And this is commonly where most conventional strategic planning initiatives spend most of their time.

> It is truly enough said, that a corporation [or institution] has no conscience, but a corporation of conscious men is a corporation with a conscience. (Thoreau, 1849, as cited in Thoreau, 1993, p. 2)

Through these three levels of planning, required results can be defined and a useful direction can be set for the institution. And institutional planning for success at each of these levels is the foundation of a system approach to decision making.

Current Results

For effective decision making, institutional leaders must be informed as to the current accomplishments and contributions of the institution, as well as those of the individuals and teams that constitute the institution. And the same is true when anyone in the institution is going to make a decision; only the scale and scope of the information required differ. This requirement of information regarding the current accomplishments (i.e., results) is a fundamental element of effective quality management. As a statistician, the "father" of quality management, Edwards Deming, realized the critical importance of data in making decisions of all kinds within an institution. From the factory workers making decisions related to the output of production lines, to the chief financial officer selecting tactics to improve the annual profits per share, data are an essential element in effectively making decisions in today's institutions. And while many aspects of the quality management approach have become historical relics in today's institutions as management trends sweep through institutions, the fundamental concept of collecting data to inform decision makers is one aspect that will be a continuing legacy of quality management.[6]

When applying the performance accomplishment system, the collection of data regarding the current accomplishments of the institution (as well as the individuals and teams that constitute the institution) is crucial for success. In an ends-focused approach to decision making we want to define *needs* as gaps in results–discrepancies between required results (what should be accomplished) and current results (what is being accomplished). Subsequently, we define *required results* as the products of practical strategic planning. And now to complete the *needs equation* we define current results by collecting extensive data regarding the accomplishments and contributions of individuals, teams, and the institution.

Performance Requirements Analysis

While the products of strategic planning should provide decision makers with a guide to the *required results* for institutional success, visioning efforts rarely provide the details necessary for making, justifying, and evaluating complex decisions at all levels of the institution. Performance indicators detail the measurable evidence necessary to demonstrate that a planned effort has achieved the desired results. The *performance requirements analysis* identifies and clarifies these criteria for success in a brief and systematic process.

Causal Analysis

As the performance requirements analysis further delineates and clarifies the objectives derived in the strategic plan, the *causal analysis* reveals and interprets the likely causes of or reasons for the gap between the current and the required accomplishments. This identification of likely causes provides the essential link between the interventions selected to close a gap in results (i.e., address a specified need) and the probability of the solution actually accomplishing the desired results. The causal analysis is, therefore, an essential process in making effective decisions. Sometimes referred to as *needs analysis* or *training needs assessment*, the causal analysis provides the supporting data for making selections among solution alternatives (e.g., distance education).

Solution Alternatives Analysis

Each of the previous steps in applying the performance accomplishment system has focused exclusively on the results and consequences of the institutional (and individual) processes and activities. During the *solution alternatives analysis,* for the first time, decision makers weigh the many options (e.g., distance education, computer technologies, year-long schooling). Each option (or set of options) can thus be considered based on its ability to achieve the required results (defined by the performance requirements analysis) as well as its capability to address the likely causes (defined by the causal analysis). Further, since solution selection is connected to strategic planning and needs assessment steps, decision makers can rest assured that selected interventions are adequately linked to and aligned with the institution's vision and mission.

Weighing the positive and negatives of alternative solutions is not, however, always that easy a task. Often, little valid and reliable data are available for decision makers, and return-on-investment (ROI) analyses depend on implemented solutions for their calculations. So how do decision makers move forward in an informed manner? We suggest that a costs-consequences analysis can provide decision makers with a coarse-grain estimate of the cost related to closing a gap in results (i.e., meeting a need) versus the costs of not closing a gap in results (i.e., not meeting a need), the latter being a traditionally forgotten element of the decision-making process. Based on this analysis, decision makers can utilize at least approximation data when making difficult choices.

By applying this system approach to decision making, selecting the *right* solution for an institution–for example, a distance education initiative–can be accomplished in a rational and justifiable manner. But the role of decision maker doesn't necessarily end when the decision is made.

Implementation and Continuous Improvement

Even after the decision to implement a distance education solution has been made, the role of the decision maker is not complete. Throughout the implementation process, the decision maker should remain involved with the application of any distance education initiative. Continued involvement offers three benefits for the decision maker and his/her institution. The first is that the decision maker can evaluate the achievements of the solution against the performance requirements identified throughout the application of the performance accomplishment system. Second, the decision maker should be involved in future decisions regarding the continuous improvement of the selected solution.

As alterations and improvements to the selected solution are made, the initial decision maker should remain involved to preserve the linkages to required results and valuable contributions. Lastly, by remaining involved with the implementation of a distance education initiative, the decision maker can remain informed and reduce the amount of new data that will be required for effectively making future decisions.

ASKING AND ANSWERING THE RIGHT QUESTIONS

The performance accomplishment system may be used in determining the answers to a variety of difficult decisions and in making value-added contributions to your institution, clients, and clients' clients. The performance accomplishment framework will assist you in aligning the information you know about current performance with what is necessary for performance to lead to long-term success. Yet, to be successful, we must not only have an appropriate framework for answering difficult questions, but, additionally, we must ensure that we are asking the *right* questions in the first place. Doing otherwise would be similar to buying a prize-winning horse, only to find out that the game is water polo.

As decision makers in institutions, we often only know a very little about the many activities that are going on around us every day: What is Jane's department doing with this semester registrations? How is John's team handling the newest software innovations of our competitors? Has Mary's division shipped their products to the clients in Asia yet? And in many cases, we know even less about the contributions and results being accomplished by the many individuals, teams, and units of our institution: What were the results of Jane's department switching to online registration last year? Did the software released by John's team meet the requirements of our clients in their efforts to boost their profits? What is the safety record of clients using the products shipped by Mary's division?

At first glance, you may say, "Yes, but that is the responsibility of the president, principal, or CEO–not me." Or your initial reaction may be, "But that is why we have those annual retreats, to make sure everyone is on the same page." And yet, when applying a system approach to decision making, we cannot afford to ignore any subsystem. To ignore other subsystems for the sole success of our subsystem would constitute sub-optimization, and put the success of the entire system in jeopardy.

So, how can we ensure the success of the system without having to involve everyone in the institution in every decision that has to be made? We start by ensuring that we are asking the right questions.

The questions we ask, and the answers we find, provide the necessary strategic alignment to effectively apply the performance accomplishment system in our decision making. In *Strategic Thinking* (1998, p. 203), Kaufman offers the following questions as guidelines for achieving strategic alignment:

> Do you commit to deliver institutional contributions that add value for your external clients AND society, now and in the future?

> Do you commit to deliver contributions that have the quality required by your institution and its external partners?

Do you commit to produce internal results that have the quality required by your internal partners, individually and in teams?

Do you commit to have efficient internal products, programs, projects, and activities?

Do you commit to create and ensure the quality and appropriateness of the human, capital, and physical resources available?

Do you commit to deliver:

  a: products, activities, methods, and procedures that have positive value and worth?

  b: the results and accomplishments defined by our objectives?

An honest answer of "yes" to all of these questions requires that each of us consider our current motivations and reasons for commitment. Too often, today's motivations are focused on getting more computers, increasing standardized test scores, increasing training enrollments, and other means and resource variables alone. Yet, if we are committed to the achievement of success with regard to each question, then the achievement of useful results is our vision and our institution's vision.[7] On the other hand, if we don't or can't answer "yes" to these questions, who will?

Strategic alignment is only attained in institutional decision making when the answer to each of these questions is "yes." When you, and your institution, have committed to the delivery of results that add value for external clients and society, you have committed to taking a system approach to decision making. And this commitment to making useful contributions sets the guiding direction for all decision making within the institution.

Having a useful (and utilized) *north star* for guiding decisions within an institution can prevent sub-optimization by ensuring that all divisions, departments, teams, and individuals have the same overarching objective in mind. And this is how we can attain strategic alignment without having to know the specifics of what is being accomplished in all areas of our institution.

So what are your answers to the questions posed? What are your institution's answers?

By establishing clear answers to these essential questions, you can calibrate the likely success of most institutional efforts and develop strategic alliances with others to work toward useful results. Additionally, you can adjust your decision making to account for departments or individuals that may be making decisions that are not aligned with the committed objectives of the institution (while working to bring them onboard with the objectives of the institution).

CONCLUSION

In today's educational environment, making the "right" decisions regarding distance education can be critical for the long-term success of an institution. But making the "right" decisions begins with determining what long-term success indicators will be used later to judge those decisions. This article offers a framework for making difficult decisions that is based on a system approach that aligns planning at the mega, macro, and micro levels. The goals and objectives at each of these levels can assist institutions in establishing the long-term indicators of success that can provide direction in decision making. By utilizing this framework, decision makers can answer difficult questions and maintain the necessary alignments with the direction and vision of the institution.

NOTES

1. If your institution has already determined that distance education is the right solution, you may want to review Watkins and Kaufman (2002).

2. Initially proposed by Doug Leigh and later included in Kaufman, Watkins, and Leigh, 2001.

3. An example of a mega level objective would be "a world where everyone is self-sufficient and self-reliant" (see Kaufman, Watkins, & Leigh, 2001).

4. An example of a macro level objective would be "a community where no individual is debilitated by substance or person abuse" (see Kaufman, Watkins, & Leigh, 2001).

5. An example of a micro level objective would be that "all students will have the mathematics skills required to obtain employment" (see Kaufman, Watkins, & Leigh, 2001).

6. We suggest that it was likely the misapplication of Deming's quality principles that led to its lackluster success in many U.S. institutions.

7. Linked to and aligned with an ideal vision stating the kind of world we are committed to creating for future generations.

REFERENCES

BrainyMedia.com (2002). Brainy quotes. Retrieved June 27, 2002, from http://www.brainyquote.com/quotes/quotes/f/q107124.html/

Drucker, P. F. (1993). *Post-capitalist society*. New York: HarperBusiness.

Haeckel, S. (1999). *Adaptive enterprise: Creating and leading sense-and-respond organizations*. Boston: Harvard Business School Press.

Kaufman, R., Oakley-Brown, H., Watkins, R., & Leigh, D. (2003). *Strategic planning for success: Aligning people, performance, and payoffs*. San Francisco: Jossey-Bass.

Kaufman, R., Watkins, R., & Leigh, D. (2001). *Useful educational results: Defining, prioritizing and achieving*. Lancaster, PA: Proactive Publishing.

Kaufman, R., Watkins, R., & Guerra, I. (2001). The future of distance education: Defining and sustaining useful results. *Educational Technology, 41*(3), 19-26.

Kaufman, R. (2000). *Mega planning: Practical tools for organizational success.* Thousand Oaks, CA: Sage Publications.

Kaufman, R. (1998). *Strategic thinking: A guide to identifying and solving problems.* Arlington, VA., & Washington, DC: Jointly published by the American Society for Training & Development and the International Society for Performance Improvement.

Kaufman, R., Stith, M., Triner, D., & Watkins, R. (1998). The changing corporate mind: Organizations, vision, mission, purposes, and indicators on the move toward societal payoffs. *Performance Improvement Quarterly, 11*(3), 32-34.

Kaufman, R. (1992). *Strategic planning plus: An organizational guide. (Revised).* Newbury Park, CA: Sage.

Kaufman, R., & Watkins, R. (2000). Getting serious about results and payoffs: We are what we say, do, and deliver. *Performance Improvement, 39*(4), 23-32.

Kaufman, R. (2000). *Mega planning: Practical tools for organizational success.* Thousand Oaks, CA: Sage Publications.

Thoreau, H. D. (1993). *Civil disobedience and other essays (unabridged).* Mineola, NY: Dover Publications.

Watkins, R., & Kaufman, R. (2002). Is your distance education program going to accomplish useful results? In M. Silberman (Ed.), *The 2002 training and performance sourcebook*, pp. 89-96. Princeton, NJ: McGraw Hill.

Watkins, R., & Kaufman, R. (in press). Strategic planning for distance education. In M. Moore (in press*). Handbook of American distance education.*

Watkins, R., Leigh, D., Platt, W., & Kaufman, R. (1998). Needs assessment: A digest, review, and comparison of needs assessment literature. *Performance Improvement, 37*(7), 40-53.

Cleborne D. Maddux

Fads, Distance Education, and the Importance of Theory

SUMMARY. Fads are common in every area of education. The problem with fads is that even promising developments are quickly abandoned to make room for the next innovation. Educational innovations become fads partly because they are without a firm foundation in theories of learning, or because that foundation is not fully identified and communicated. There have been many examples of fads in information technology in education. The question of whether or not distance education will turn out to be a fad is addressed, and some tentative steps are discussed that might help avoid its achieving fad status. *[Article copies available for a fee from The Haworth Document Delivery Service: 1-800-HAWORTH. E-mail address: <docdelivery@ haworthpress.com> Website: <http://www.HaworthPress.com> © 2003 by The Haworth Press, Inc. All rights reserved.]*

KEYWORDS. Fads, distance education, information technology in education, educational theory, future of higher education

As we are all painfully aware, education in general, and information technology in education in particular, are highly prone to fads. From its inception, in-

CLEBORNE D. MADDUX is Associate Editor for Research, *Computers in the Schools*, and Professor, University of Nevada, Reno, Department of Counseling and Educational Psychology, Reno, NV 89557 (E-mail: maddux@unr.edu).

[Haworth co-indexing entry note]: "Fads, Distance Education, and the Importance of Theory." Maddux, Cleborne D. Co-published simultaneously in *Computers in the Schools* (The Haworth Press, Inc.) Vol. 20, No. 3, 2003, pp. 121-127; and: *Distance Education: What Works Well* (ed: Michael Corry, and Chih-Hsiung Tu) The Haworth Press, Inc., 2003, pp. 121-127. Single or multiple copies of this article are available for a fee from The Haworth Document Delivery Service [1-800-HAWORTH, 9:00 a.m. - 5:00 p.m. (EST). E-mail address: docdelivery@haworthpress.com].

10.1300/J025v20n03_11
121

formation technology in education has been marked by repetitive cycles of (a) infatuation with an innovation, (b) unrealistically optimistic expectations for that innovation, (c) disillusionment with the innovation when it proves not to be an educational panacea, and (d) rapid abandonment of the innovation. This cycle, which might be termed the *Educational Pendulum Syndrome* (Maddux, 1986, 1990; Maddux & Cummings, in press), then begins anew with some other innovation in the spotlight.

The problem with fads is not so much their *arrival*, but the timing of their *departure*, which tends to be premature. We are well rid of some of the fads that have plagued the field of information technology in education in the past. However, the Pendulum Syndrome is damaging because some of the innovations that are subject to it are useful, or promising, but, because they are fads, these are abandoned just as quickly as less promising developments. In other words, fad status results in both premature adoption and premature abandonment.

Only a few of the fads we have experienced in information technology in education are drill-and-practice software, the student-to-computer-ratio, computer literacy, BASIC programming for all students, simulations, equity, authoring systems, expert systems, artificial intelligence, Logo as a cognitive amplifier, integrated learning systems, partnerships with business and industry, and wireless networks (Maddux, in press). Most of the innovations in this list have already suffered partial or complete abandonment in schools, although some, such as the Logo programming language, were effective, or promising. Indeed, research has since shown that, under the right circumstances, Logo *can* be effective as a cognitive amplifier. Nevertheless, Logo has been abandoned in U.S. schools, save for a few isolated districts and schools that house the small and continually shrinking corps of die-hard advocates who continue to use it.

The most recent hot topics in information technology in education include the Internet, the World Wide Web, postmodernism, constructivism, qualitative research, WebQuests, electronic portfolios, personal digital assistants (PDAs), and distance education (Maddux, in press). Only time will tell which of these innovations will, by their rapid abandonment, prove to be only the most recent educational fads.

The Internet and the World Wide Web are special cases that are unlikely to disappear from schools because they are so ubiquitous and because they have become so important in every walk of life. The same can be said for computers in general. Although computers were once at considerable risk of abandonment in education, their acceptance in the culture at large and worldwide is so sweeping and absolute that they are no longer in danger of being excluded from schools.

The same cannot be said for postmodernism, constructivism, and qualitative research, which, I believe, are very much in danger of suffering the fate of all educational fads. However, the current educational popularity of these topics is part of a general societal movement to reject facts, absolute truths, science and scientific thinking, and to embrace subjectivity and relativity as the basis of all knowledge. Indeed, Constas (1998) suggests that postmodernism rejects *reason* itself, and views reason as monstrous.

Additionally, both postmodernism and constructivism, as currently articulated in the educational literature, are, in my view, symptoms of a spreading anti-intellectualism among academics in fields that are often (ironically) called the *social sciences*. Although this is not the place to fully explore this idea, which some will find controversial, suffice it to say that some of the best evidence for anti-intellectualism in the current educational preoccupation with postmodernism and constructivism is that there is so little agreement in the educational literature about how to define these terms.

Constas (1998) has referred to the multiplicity of definitions of postmodernism as "labyrinthine" (p. 36), and suggests the educational literature is full of debate about whether or not it is even possible, or desirable, to define it (e.g., Codrington, 1998). Some postmodern writers even take the position that a desire for clarity about postmodernism, or clarity about *any* theory, is an inappropriate goal, and is merely part of the "humanist romance of knowledge as cure" (Lather, 1996, p. 539).

The definition of constructivism is also obscure. In a previous article in this journal (Maddux & Cummings, 1999), it was mentioned that there is little agreement about definition, and the educational literature refers to constructivism with a wide variety of descriptors, including, among many others, a *philosophy*, an *attitude*, a *methodology*, an *approach*, a *model*, an *epistemology*, a *framework*, and a *theory*. Among these, the idea that constructivism is a *theory* seems to be the most popular, even though, at best, it appears to be only a general term or concept "loosely and often haphazardly derived from a variety of theories in developmental psychology" (Maddux, & Cummings, 1999, p. 7). That article went on to suggest that constructivism has outlived its usefulness as an educational term, since it seems to mean all things to all people, and is thus useless as a descriptor.

Thus, both postmodernism and constructivism seem to be prime candidates for fad status and consequent hasty abandonment. It seems to me that these two ideas can be used to illustrate one of the important reasons why innovations become fads. They become fads partly because they are *theoretically impoverished* (Maddux & Cummings, in press). I believe it is almost inevitable that an innovation will become a fad if (a) the innovation lacks a coherent and logical foundation in a theory or theories of learning or (b) if advocates fail to properly understand and communicate this foundation as part of their advocacy. It is this latter situation that seems to me to be the case with both postmodernism and constructivism. There *are* strong theoretical foundations for both these ideas, but educational advocates have not done a good job of finding them, understanding them, and communicating them clearly to colleagues.

Theoretical impoverishment dooms an innovation to failure and abandonment because theory is the only practical guide for the successful use of an innovation, and the only source of clues for how the implementation might be modified if it fails to be successful in some specific educational environment or with specific kinds or ages of learners. Since, by the definition above, both postmodernism and constructivism are theoretically impoverished, they are unlikely to lead to successful educational implementation, and are likely, therefore, to be quickly abandoned.

Qualitative research is another innovation in information technology in education that is likely to fall prey to the Pendulum Syndrome. Again, there *are* theoretical connections for qualitative research, but those connections seem to be poorly understood by many educational advocates. Actually, there is nothing new about qualitative research, and such techniques are completely legitimate and useful in certain research situations. However, in my opinion, many of the extremists who advocate complete abandonment of quantitative research strategies in preference for qualitative ones, do so not for carefully articulated theoretical reasons, but because they seem to believe that qualitative research will relieve them of the need for the kind of careful advance planning followed by care and structure in data gathering and analysis that is characteristic of quantitative research strategies. Others appear to suffer from math anxiety and embrace qualitative strategies because they wish to avoid the number concepts and statistical calculations necessary to treat data quantitatively. Motivations such as these are, in my opinion, unlikely to lead to research studies and findings that are valid and useful. Therefore, I believe that the near-fanatical, extremist advocacy of qualitative research that is currently prevalent in information technology in education is unlikely to be popular for much longer.

Webquests, electronic portfolios, and personal digital assistants *(PDAs)* also seem prime candidates for fad status, since they either lack a theoretical orientation, or because many advocates and practitioners are ignoring theoretical connections that do exist. Space does not permit a full discussion of all three of these innovations, but interested readers are referred to Maddux and Cummings (in press).

This brings me to distance education, and the question of whether or not distance education is simply one more educational fad. Like the Internet and the Web (and perhaps because of distance education's ability to make use of the Internet and the Web), distance education seems to me to be a special case. Like the Internet and the Web, the educational benefits of distance education have been oversold and exploited–but, like the Internet and the Web, distance education, I believe, is not likely to disappear. Rather, there is every indication that its use will continue to grow. More and more students will take advantage of distance education, and its growth is likely to extend beyond higher education to public secondary education, and perhaps even to middle and elementary school levels.

That may be good news for advocates of distance education. Unfortunately, I think there is also some related, bad news. It seems to me that the growth of distance education has mushroomed completely out of control and shows every sign of continuing to do so. There are many reasons why this has happened, including the very real added convenience for students as well as the worldwide fascination with computer hardware and software. However, I believe the most important and ominous reason for distance education's meteoric rise in popularity and availability is *economic* in nature. While it is becoming clear that high-quality distance education programs are, in the final analysis, no less expensive for the institutions that offer them than are traditional educational offerings, the critical economic point may be that distance education opens up a new, huge, and previously untapped market of potential students who have been unwilling or unable to make use of traditional campus services. This fact, coupled with declining public financial support for higher education, and the consequent, ongoing nationwide commercialization of higher education, ensures the continued proliferation of distance education.

Two things seem clear: (a) distance education is not going away, and (b) public institutions *must* participate because private institutions are rushing to do so, and public institutions, as we all know, are desperate for revenue. Hardly a week goes by that I do not receive at least one slick, four-color brochure, usually from a private institution, but increasingly also from public ones, offering professional certificate programs, bachelor's, master's, and even doctoral degrees in a variety of disciplines, delivered entirely online with absolutely no requirement for physical attendance on any campus.

While many of us find these offerings to be unfortunate to say the least, there is no practical advantage to be had in whining among ourselves about diploma mills and the ethics of the purchased degree. Diploma mills exist, as they have for many years. Their programs exist and they are not going away.

I believe that our challenge is not to destroy these institutions and their programs (we couldn't if we tried), but neither is it to duplicate their methods to earn a quick dollar. The challenge will be to implement distance education in a thoughtful, ethical way, and to do so always with the goal of delivering the best possible education, rather than making the largest possible profit. That approach sounds easy to adopt and maintain, but the pressure to adopt the profit motive is immense and growing daily. That pressure comes from higher education administrators who are increasingly subscribing to the business maxims that (a) the customer is always right, and (b) higher education is merely another commodity to be bought and sold. In the short term and from a pragmatic point of view, these administrators may be correct, but I am still enough of an idealist to believe that in the long term, the quality of what is offered *will* make a difference. If traditional education has anything to offer, as I believe it does, then employers will eventually recognize the difference in the expertise of those who have purchased their degrees and those who have earned them. Most students will also eventually recognize the difference. Most have done so in the past with regard to a variety of long-standing diploma mills, and I believe most will do so in the future with regard to the increasing numbers of online diploma mills.

That is not to imply that distance offerings are uniformly of poorer quality than traditional offerings. Far from it–there are many courses and perhaps portions of entire programs that are well suited to online delivery. And therein lies the challenge–the challenge of preserving what is best about our traditional offerings while incorporating the best from distance education. We must continue to make the point that there is no reason why distance education cannot *supplement* traditional education rather than *replace* it. We must then set about investigating the teacher\learner\treatment interactions that will enable us to make the best use of distance education in combination with traditional approaches. We must insist that implementation of distance education policies and procedures not be theoretically impoverished. Rather, they must be based on theories of teaching and learning, and they must acknowledge the importance of learning not just the knowledge and skills, but also the *culture* of a discipline.

In the last few years, there have been some highly pessimistic predictions about what is going to happen to traditional higher education as a result of distance education. Noble (1998), for example, has said, "In ten years, we will look upon the wired remains of our once great democratic higher education system and wonder how we let it happen" (p. 40). I believe the answer to that question will be that we couldn't *prevent* it from happening.

The open question, however, is what "it" will turn out to be. The many doomsayers notwithstanding, I, for one, do not believe that higher education as we know it will be destroyed. There will always be university campuses and students who desire to experience them, especially at the undergraduate level. The future of graduate education is more problematic, but even there I am optimistic. I believe we will rise to the occasion. Like all great trials, the present problem may have a positive side to it. We all realize that traditional higher education is not perfect, and there is much about it that can be improved. Distance education in general, and even the online diploma mills themselves, may provide the force needed to overcome the considerable inertia present in higher education and bring about some positive changes. I believe this will be so.

REFERENCES

Codrington, G. (1998). *Generation X: WHO, what, why and where to?* Retrieved October 9, 2002, from http://www.youth.co.za/genxthesis/intro.htm

Constas, M. A. (1998). Deciphering postmodern educational research. *Educational Researcher, 27*(9), 36-42.

Lather, P. (1996). Troubling clarity: The politics of accessible language. *Harvard Educational Review, 66*(3), 525-554.

Laudan, L. (1990). *Science and relativism.* Chicago, IL: University of Chicago Press.

Maddux, C. D. (1986). The educational computing backlash: Can the swing of the pendulum be halted? *Computers in the Schools, 3*(2), 27-30.

Maddux, C. D. (1990). The qualitative/quantitative research debate: Extremism and the educational pendulum. *Computers in the Schools, 7*(3), 35-45.

Maddux, C. D. (in press). Twenty years of research in information technology in education: Assessing our progress. *Computers in the Schools.*

Maddux, C. D., & Cummings, R. (1999). Constructivism: Has the term outlived its usefulness? *Computers in the Schools, 15*(3/4), 5-20.

Maddux, C. D., & Cummings, R. (in press). Fad, fashion, and the weak role of theory and research in information technology in education. *Journal of Research on Technology in Education.*

Noble, D. F. (1998). Selling academe to the technology industry. *Thought and Action, 14*(1), 29-40.

Index